GUIDANCE MONOGRAPH SERIES

SHELLEY C. STONE

BRUCE SHERTZER

Editors

GUIDANCE MONOGRAPH SERIES

The general purpose of Houghton Mifflin's Guidance Monograph Series is to provide high quality coverage of topics which are of abiding importance in contemporary counseling and guidance practice. In a rapidly expanding field of endeavor, change and innovation are inevitably present. A trend accompanying such growth is greater and greater specialization. Specialization results in an increased demand for materials which reflect current modifications in guidance practice while simultaneously treating the field in greater depth and detail than commonly found in textbooks and brief journal articles.

The list of eminent contributors to this series assures the reader expert treatment of the areas covered. The monographs are designed for consumers with varying familiarity to the counseling and guidance field. The editors believe that the series will be useful to experienced practitioners as well as beginning students. While these groups may use the monographs with somewhat different goals in mind, both will benefit from the treatment given to content areas.

The content areas treated have been selected because of specific criteria. Among them are timeliness, practicality, and persistency of the issues involved. Above all, the editors have attempted to select topics which are of major substantive concern to counseling and guidance personnel.

Shelley C. Stone

Bruce Shertzer

CONTROVERSIAL ISSUES IN TESTING

JAMES R. BARCLAY

CALIFORNIA STATE COLLEGE AT HAYWARD

HOUGHTON MIFFLIN COMPANY · BOSTON

NEW YORK · ATLANTA · GENEVA, ILL. · DALLAS · PALO ALTO

CONTENTS

v

EDITORS' INTRODUCTION

During the 1960's psychological and educational testing and those who use tests have borne the brunt of much acrimony. In the mid-1960's those who rely on tests to varying degrees in their work found themselves defending their practices against many types of critics, some knowledgeable and some amazingly naïve. In the heat generated by such attacks, and the defenses it evoked, the larger context which nurtured the battle and served as the more pertinent base for those who fought tended to be overlooked. Dr. Barclay's monograph compellingly draws us back from the morass of petty bickering, ineffectual charges and countercharges to the solid ground of the social context in which tests are created, used, and sometimes abused.

Professor Barclay's discussion focuses on what he appropriately perceives as the core problems: for what purpose testing is done and what constitutes meaningful criteria of effective human behavior. It is within the framework of the social use and relevance of tests that a worthwhile confrontation between protagonists can occur.

Much value is to be gained from studying the material presented in this monograph. Its value lies in the broad sweep implicit in the author's approach which obliges one to view testing from a broad rather than a narrow base and thereby permits one to derive greater meaning and understanding of the basic issues presented.

SHELLEY C. STONE

BRUCE SHERTZER

The Popular Attack on Testing and Counseling: An Overview

It has been apparent for some time that a major attack is being made on the testing movement. From a variety of sources some severe charges are being lodged against the consulting psychologist, the counselor, the school personnel worker, and the professional user of tests. In the past few years there have been a number of articles and books written attacking testing on various levels. There have also been some excellent defenses of testing in the literature of journals. These attacks on testing have extended not only to projective techniques and objective test questions, but to the use of personality testing in the schools, the selection procedures of business, and achievement type tests given as entrance batteries for colleges and universities.

Representative of this literature are the following articles and books which may provide a sample of the kinds of criticisms which have been enunciated:

1) "Brain picking in the school" (*Human Events*, Section 4, November 17, 1962);
2) "The Infamous Blackie Cartoons" (*American Capsule News*, September 15, 1962);

3) "A Note on the Technology of Cynicism" by Donald Barr (*Columbia University Forum,* Summer 1963);

4) A local column by Pierre Pulling in the (Intermountain), an Idaho Weekly Newspaper, Volumn 12, No. 43, November 7, 1963;

5) An article by Fred H. Hechinger, Education Editor of the *New York Times,* entitled: "Test Question," (Sunday, October 27, 1963);

6) The book *The Brain Watchers* written by Martin J. Gross (Random House, 1962).

The Criticisms

Included in these samples are two publications from conservative sources. Barr's article appeared in a professional journal, and Hechinger's article appeared in the education section of the New York Times, Sunday Edition. Pulling's column was typical of small town columnists throughout the country insofar as many local papers do carry columns of this general commentary nature. Finally, the book by Gross represented a major effort to "expose" commercial testing agencies.

What do these articles and this book say? The article on "brain picking" is written by a U. S. Congressman, Representative John Ashbrook. After citing a number of objectionable items from some group tests, he states that questions which probe at attitudes towards parents, the Bible, or patriotism plant the seeds of doubt in the minds of youth. He states further that these tests are devised arbitrarily and sold under the seal of scientific infallibility. He quotes Dr. Chisholm, former Director-General of the World Health Organization, as stating that sin and the subjective conviction of sin are the arch-enemies of mental health and progress. Finally, Congressman Ashbrook lumps Freudian psychiatry, UNESCO, and brain picking tests together as being part of a subversive plot "to detect and indoctrinate." He states categorically that the Dewey or Horace Mann approach to education is tied up with testing and these other movements in an attempt to undermine the traditional values of American democracy and make it easy for America to eventually swing into the Marxist-Communist orbit.

This same line of approach, but in a much more vitriolic manner, is pursued by *American Capsule News.* Here the question of the Blacky Picture Test is taken up. Several testing projects in Wichita,

Kansas, and Seattle, Washington, were mentioned.[1] This is what was written:

> The Reds prepared a panel of 12 cartoons for the Seattle 'project.' These were passed on to teachers, who must be either sex degenerates or sex perverts, to innoculate the minds of their pupils with. The little victims were told to write down what (erotic) thoughts each cartoon put in their heads. Not even the degenerate Freud, with his parential [sic!] incest complex, could have thought up anything as rotten as this 'test.'

The balance of the article is concerned with an "expose" of the Blacky Picture Test.

A third article which is reviewed here is not in any way written in the same vein as the above two. This is a rather popular approach to difficulties in multiple-choice tests. The author, Dr. Donald Barr, is assistant Dean of the Faculty of Engineering and Applied Science at Columbia University. He attacks multiple-choice tests in American education. He singles out the Scholastic Aptitude Test, the College Entrance Examination Boards, and a variety of others. He particularly attacks the large corporations who are making money on these tests, but he also returns to the conflict-in-values theme which is indicated in the other two articles. Without alluding to a "plot" to undermine the morals of American youth, he does point up some particular items in tests such as the Minnesota Multiphasic Test of Personality which could create conflict situations in the minds of people who believe in such things as the "second coming of Christ."

The fourth article is of purely local interest but may be typical of many columnists who are looking for a good "popular" theme. This article was written by Pierre Pulling, a retired professor of Biology at Idaho State University. Mr. Pulling rambled on about testing being

---

[1] One of the tests or surveys which inspired a good deal of opposition was a document entitled: "Kansas Junior High School Student Survey." This survey was conducted by the University of Kansas Bureau of Child Research in two Wichita junior high schools among students of both sexes, ranging from 11 to 14 years of age. This questionnaire consisted of some 200 items which ask questions such as:
Would you: 1. Steal goods from warehouses or storage houses?
        2. Steal more than $2 from your parents?
        3. Fight physically and bodily with an adult relative?
True or False — I have gone further than petting with a person of the opposite sex. I have answered ads in comic books or other magazines which advertised pictures, photographs, or stories about sexual matters.
In addition, one section of the test was entitled "Rules We All Break." In this section, children were informed of means of stealing property, damaging cemetery property, destroying road markers, siphoning gas from cars, puncturing tires and similar ideas. (Congressional Record, 1961).

similar to phrenology. He said that his article was occasioned by a desultory contact with *some* child who took *some* test at *some* time in *some* place and was not rated too bright in mathematics. Nonetheless, this particular individual went to *some* college *somewhere* and *somehow* succeeded, all of which proves beyond the shadow of a doubt in Mr. Pulling's logic that *all* testing in *all* places and on *all* levels is similar to the cephalic index of the phrenologists. He further stated that he had always had a confused impression of testing and that prospective students at Idaho State University at one time took "IQ" tests. He obviously here mixed up percentile norms on an achievement battery with "IQ" scores. Observing that he had never looked at test rosters routinely, he clinched his whole argument by relevant memory flashbacks of what education was like in the private schools of upper New York at the end of the last century.

The article by Fred Hechinger simply reports research done by Dr. Benno G. Fricke, Assistant Chief of the Evaluation and Examinations Division of the University of Michigan's Bureau of Psychological Services. Dr. Fricke's conclusions are about the College Board Examinations and the Scholastic Aptitude Tests. The objections appear to be well couched and indicate that many aptitude tests measure only general academic ability rather than specific achievement in specific areas. Dr. Fricke's objections center on the fact that the Scholastic Aptitude Tests are inbred in that when new items are selected they are designed to measure the same old things as the former items. He suggests that specific examinations be given in each subject matter field.

The book by Martin Gross makes interesting reading. Page after page of information is provided about the use of aptitude testing and projective techniques by big business. Example after example is provided to illustrate the techniques used. One chapter speaks of the school counselor and school psychologist. He criticizes school counselors as untrained people or classroom teachers who have taken a few courses and have "empathy." He suggests that counselors use tests in order to find "something" to talk to students about. "In most cases, guidance people are woefully untrained to handle the proper interpretation of personality tests, a job as we have seen — that is nearly, if not actually, impossible for the Ph. D. psychologist." Mr. Gross documents many of his statements by references to specific schools or corporations where problems existed. He winds up his discussion by an examination of whether tests are scientific or mythological.

The Issues

From these articles and the book reviewed it would appear that certain issues are the basis of these criticisms. Though the particular reports may be exaggerated or the logic of generalization faulty, the issues would seem to be the following:

1. That counseling practice and the use of testing is a Communist-inspired plot to subvert and pervert the morals of American youth.
2. That testing is being misused by many so-called professionals and some individuals who are far from being professional.
3. That some tests are personally obnoxious to certain segments of the population and contain items which actually inform children of anti-social or law-breaking conduct.
4. That the prediction from some of these tests is nearly null for individuals.
5. That there has been a widespread "invasion" of personal rights through the use of certain types of tests and the dissemination of these test results.

These allegations regarding testing should be considered one by one to determine whether or not the charges are valid. The first one suggests that the entire counseling and testing movement is of a "pinko" nature and is directly or indirectly inspired by Communism. This is pure nonsense. Morover, the attempt to draw John Dewey and even Horace Mann into this plot is ludicrous to the extreme. What are these charges really aimed at? It would seem that they are directed towards those in the schools who view the school as an agent of cultural transmission. From this frame of reference, educators and counselors believe that it is necessary to acquaint children not only with what has been traditionally passed on, but to prepare them to assess and evaluate new developments in our technological culture. This view is particularly disturbing to those elements in our society who believe that our culture is deteriorating and who see the true path as one in which the schools reinforce and teach only those traditional values which have been held in the past or are thought to have been held in the past. These conservatives would wish the school to function solely as a transmitter of that information and those values to which the conservatives subscribe. They have difficulty valuing the exploration of the consequences of divergent thinking in certain areas of the social and behavioral sciences. Are they not really seeking some kind of absolute criterion whereby all learning processes can be monitored and referred to the "correct" solutions? Is it possible to utilize either exaggerated patriotism or some other set of absolute values as a criterion of education in a pluralistic society?

Another set of issues appears to be directed at the misuse of tests by individuals and groups. Surely there is ground for these allegations. There have been many misuses of testing and test results. Most specifically, those who use tests have come to believe in the test score as a kind of absolute. The gist of the charges made against testing and the use of tests does appear to be founded in some very real abuses. We need to recognize that some items in some tests are personally obnoxious to certain segments of the population. Moreover, on occasions individuals who have been unqualified to use restricted tests have used them. Again, school counselors have often used group achievement and personality tests as material to be discussed with students and their parents without mentioning the important considerations regarding the standard error of measurement. The allegation has been made also that many test items referring to personality constructs are formulated from a psychoanalytic viewpoint in which religion specifically is considered to be a form of adolescent psychopathology. This would appear to be a valid complaint. A discussion on the nature of sin held several years ago brought this matter out into clear focus (Mowrer, Ellis, Curran, & Shoben, 1960). Albert Ellis held that there was no room for the concept of sin in psychotherapy. Others, however, such as Hobart Mowrer, called for a re-examination of the entire area of guilt and sin in terms of psychotherapy. In view of the fact that many of the test items for instruments such as the MMPI, the California Test of Personality, or other such tests presumably have a psychoanalytic bias, it is understandable that certain items may be personally obnoxious.

There are many types of tests and many varieties of testers. Testing in any form is a scientific attempt to measure some aspect of behavior, achievement, personality, or learning. Teacher-made tests which are used by every teacher possess no real reliability or validity except in terms of the teacher himself. These tests ordinarily measure whether a given student has learned to repeat the information which a teacher deems important or whether a student can organize his material in such a way that it conforms to the design of the teacher. Standardized tests, on the other hand, are usually composed by individuals who are deemed to have some expert knowledge in the field under consideration. Certain items are selected and tested to learn whether they do measure whatever the characteristic may be. Once complex areas of developmental variance, environmental differences, and adequate sampling have been worked out, large populations are included in the norming process. By item analysis the content of the test is screened and reanalyzed. The entire approach is based on a statistical theory relating to large populations and the assumption of normality of distribution. The end result of the test is to provide a measure of some characteristic either in the area of personality, learning, or achievement. Prediction is never postulated of individuals and is seldom postulated of populations without considerable qualifying remarks. Finally, tests of this nature seldom specify anything about motivation, creativity, or those other intangible personal factors which often spell the difference between success and failure. Thus, a test result does not imply that a given individual is predestined in some quasi-theological manner to the heaven of success, the hell of failure, or the limbo of probation.

Of even more concern are those tests known as projective techniques. The most widely known projective techniques are the Rorschach, the Thematic Apperception Test, and the sentence-completion tests. The theory behind projective techniques is basically one founded on psychoanalytic theory. Though the roots of this approach lie in phenomenology and the view that each individual structures reality in a basically unique framework, psychoanalytic theory postulates that each individual represses a good deal of his basic needs and wishes. Through the use of the interpretation of ink blots or pictures, the intent is to tap lower levels of cognition through the analysis of quantity and quality of the responses given to these stimuli. Other projective techniques such as the Blacky Pictures Test or the IES Test are frankly psychoanalytic in their design and attempt to tap specific feelings which are postulated on the basis of psychoanalytic theory.

The chief problem in the use of projective techniques centers around the interpretation of the results. Personal resistance to some of the concepts in these tests is invariably interpreted as a sign of rigidity and repressed material. This is particularly so in tests such as the Blacky Pictures Test where some of the material presented is frankly sexual in nature and can hardly be disguised. Currently lacking in the use of projective techniques are adequate, reliable, and valid norms. Generalizations about school youth which are based on norms developed in hospital settings are very precarious. The same fact would seem to be indicated by the use of these tests in industry for determining who would make a good executive.

Another issue in regard to testing seems to be focused on the problem of predictive validity. Many of the arguments against the achievement batteries and entrance tests are that they are not very good predictive instruments. The best correlations of entrance batteries in college with grade point averages range between the .60–.70 level. Obviously there are some students who are apparently low in academic promise and may end up in the upper ranks of graduating seniors. The problems are not so much related to the format or content of the test given, since we know that high grades will predict nearly as well as an entrance battery. They are more immediately related to the instability of the criterion used, *i.e.*, grade point average. Grading practices vary within the institution and between institutions, though it is likely that the grading variation within the institution between departments may be more readily approximated between universities than total comparisons. In other words, colleges of education probably grade similarly when compared from institution to institution; and certain liberal arts departments also probably are similar in grading practices.

But the problems of prediction do not stop there. There are obviously differences between high school products and their success at various institutions. Lindquist (1963) has attempted to approach this problem, but at present he feels that it is nearly a hopeless task. Moreover, when personality tests are added to entrance battery scores, the results in multiple correlation are negligible (Fishman & Pasanella, 1960).[2] The problems which face the test constructors in college entrance batteries are not so much a matter of which items should be included, but rather of how to obtain a stable, practical, and utilitarian criterion by which to measure success. This same problem besets the users of individual tests and particularly those who would use individual projective techniques which are currently available to qualified psychologists.

Re-evaluation

The questions which have been discussed in the earlier section relate to two problems specifically and call attention to a third more central question in testing. The first of these questions is 1) are these criticisms of testing justified, and if so to what extent? The second question is 2) what should be the stance of the counselor in relationship to these criticisms? Finally, both of these questions must be broadly related to the central problem itself: 3) what are the purposes of testing and how do we determine relevant and effective criteria of human behavior?

In response to the first and second questions, it should be apparent at this point that the writer believes some justifiable criticism has been leveled against the use of tests. Most of the criticisms center on the problem of poor judgment or uninformed judgments by those who use tests. Examples have been given of the use of tests which are either

---

[2] Fishman reports that nearly 500 studies have been done in predicting academic success from entrance batteries. When personality tests are added to the multiple factors the multiple correlation is increased by only .01 or .02.

inappropriate or offensive in some ways. The allegation that counselors are poorly trained and often use psychological tools in improper ways also has some truth in it. But the fact that some abuses of testing have taken place cannot alone imply that all testing methodology is wrong or that the counseling use of tests is a Communist plot.

The indictments which have been made regarding testing and counseling also point up the need for more detailed and advanced training for counselors. They underline the need for a strong network of professional identification through national, state, and local levels. The proper place to discipline unethical conduct and to impose and maintain standards is through the professional organization of counselors, the American Personnel and Guidance Association. Studies are under way by various groups in the organization to clarify the role of the counselor and to make recommendations for training and ethical standards within the profession. Accompanying this objective must be efforts on the part of the counselor-educators to do a more effective screening and evaluation of counselor-trainees. It would seem that many counselors lack a real understanding of basic psychological concepts including testing theory. From local studies done through the NDEA institutes at Idaho State University, the writer ascertained that a majority of the enrollees actively dislike statistics and do not really wish to understand testing theory (Barclay, 1963). Unless we can train individuals to understand the tests they use and to recognize that a test score is never an absolute predictor or a tool to use to ferret out additional information, it would be best that counselors not use debatable tests at all.

Counselor-trainers also need to work on a variety of other problems. Some of these are merely technical in nature, but others are much more profound. Representative of the technical problems are counselor attitudes toward referrals and what may be called, for lack of a better term, naive curiosity. Counselors are often threatened by the referral process. Often insecure and poorly trained counselors feel that a referral to someone else is an implicit acknowledgement of personal inadequacy. As a result, they will often hold on to cases until little can be done by others. In this way they damage the professional responsibility of the profession. Until counselors are trained to a much more sophisticated level than they presently are, they should make referrals whenever a child is having repeated serious problems in school which are of a long-standing nature and jeopardize the on-going process of education for other children. Curiosity-seeking is also a problem in the naive counselor. Often he probes into areas of personal concern not so much to understand as to satisfy his own needs for vicarious experience. Sometimes he will develop questionnaires or adopt tests which are represented to him through misleading advertisement as panaceas of prediction. Curiosity to pry into personal experiences is an immature aspect of psychological sophistication. In its worst aspect it is akin to voyeurism. Counselors need to recognize that this kind of prying reveals their own adolescent development and need for vicarious experience. If they have this type of need, let them read novels! Where such curiosity in the use of tests springs from a desire to do a better job, to write a thesis, or to investigate some aspect of development behavior, counselors should consult with university personnel. Whenever research of this kind is undertaken in the public schools, it should be a joint concern of both public school personnel and university faculty. The preserving of a good research climate in a community is essential if we are to utilize the community in research activities.

Another important task involving counselor education is the basic orientation which counselors take toward problems in the school. The orientation of clinical psychology, particularly the clinical psychology of the 1940's and 1950's, was toward the abnormal. The basic assumption seemed to be that a person was abnormal until proved normal. This is not to imply that this viewpoint was specifically taught as such, but rather that with the tremendous variety of diagnostic categories and the need which clinicians had to diagnose, it became a by-product of their education. This same procedure was transferred into areas of educational, school, and counseling psychology. There is no question that knowledge about abnormal people is needed, but there is a serious question as to whether the diagnostic categories of the clinician have validity outside the specific clinical settings in which they were developed. There is a parallel between procedures in law and this attitudinal posture. In continental law, which is derived ultimately from the Napoleonic and Justinian Codes, an individual is considered guilty when charged until proved innocent. In the British Common Law and the American courts, an individual is considered innocent until proved guilty. What is suggested is that our orientation be changed to recognize that the vast majority of individuals manifest abnormal adjustment symptoms on occasion. But the criterion of their efficiency is whether they can live and work meaningfully in society. When they cannot do so, they may need institutional structure and help. In the school situation, we should consider all children as normal until it is absolutely imperative to remove the child from the setting for his own good and the good of others. Labels of maladjustment and delinquency merely make it difficult to work with the child, the teacher, and the parents.

All of the foregoing then serves as a prologue to the central problem in testing which is the subject matter of the other chapters in this monograph. Test constructors and test interpreters alike must address themselves more seriously to the question of what tests are for and what they measure. For it is here that the heart of the controversy regarding testing is to be found. There are several interlocking problems. One concerns the question of what tests do or should do, and the other centers on what they measure or should measure. In the first problem there are divisions among testing experts as to the extent to which tests should be used as predictors over against simply being objective normative measures. Some feel that the central purpose of testing is to assess group differences at a given point of time. In this sense testing is chiefly a scientific observational technique allowing for the measurement of group characteristics. However, others have pointed out that test scores can be used as predictors of future achievement, adjustment, learning, or whatever the test measures. Once they *are* so used, it becomes crucial for the profession to determine what constitutes a relevant, effective, and independent criterion. The elusive criterion problem has been with testing from the beginning. Often, test scores have been used as criteria in themselves. This is not as it was determined originally, but unfortunately the aura of scientific impeccability has tended to identify test scores with criteria. Thus, for example, adjustment has come to be what an adjustment test score measures or neurosis what a neurotic test score states.

These two issues, namely, how tests should be used and what they measure, constitute the central problem in testing today. *The purpose of this monograph is not to dwell on the more superficial issues in the controversy over testing, but to probe meaningfully into the heart of the problem itself, namely the social uses of testing and ways and means to identify more relevant criteria for testing.* Surely it is true that those who use and interpret tests should be more aware of the limitations of judgment based on testing. It is also true that tests should be constructed more fairly and administered more competently, but unless real attention is given to the nature and social use of testing and the determination of more adequate criteria of effective human behavior, it is most likely that the criticisms will continue unabated.

The format of this monograph should be mentioned briefly here. Chapter 2 is concerned with the relationship of testing to culture and the social uses of tests. Chapter 3 begins a discussion of the criterion problems in testing as it may be found in the literature discussing the environmental press. Chapter 4 is concerned with ways and means of determining more relevant criteria for testing.

2

Testing and Culture

One of the major problems in the use of testing stems from an inadequate understanding of the relationship of testing to culture. Many of the critics object to the influence which testing has come to exert in our society. Morever, many test users place an inordinate amount of confidence in the results of testing. As a direct result of this overconfidence, school systems, colleges and universities, businesses, parents, teachers, and children have all been influenced by the results of testing programs. These social consequences of testing are felt in almost every town and city of the United States. They are a significant factor in decisions made by colleges and universities in admitting students. They determine, in some instances, to which "track" a student will be assigned in high school. They are used as normative comparisons for school administrators as they look at the achievement scores for various classrooms and schools. Tests also play an important role in clinics and mental hospitals, as well as in business, for evaluating the achievement, intelligence, and personality of many different kinds of people. Though there are specific areas of concern about each kind of test and the dimensions within which testing is used, the overall problem is the use of testing itself, assumptions which underly this usage, and the impact which testing has on the structure and functions of our culture.

The Nature of Testing

Testing is a modern procedure devised to provide information about behavior in an objective and standardized manner. It is based on assumptions of measurement theory and scientific philosophy. The assumptions which are made hold that though there are individual differences in a population of people, the vast majority of these individuals do perceive reality in a similar fashion. This assumption has been identified in the past as the correspondence postulate. It is the fundamental basis for the development of scientific information. Generally it assumes a constancy of perception between individuals in relationship to perception. Obviously, there would appear to be many individual variations, but for the most part individuals can agree on their perception of phenomena. This does not mean that perceptions are not shaded with individual meaning and emotional tonality, but rather that there is a certain objective content in individual perception which is held in common with the perceptions of others who are not structurally or functionally handicapped. Thus, for example, five people may look at a Cadillac automobile. They will all see the automobile (assuming normal functioning perception), but the meaning that perception may have for each is different. One may wish to have the car, while another may dislike Cadillacs, etc. Another example might be five individuals looking at a mountain. All see the objective reality, but one may view it through the eyes of a poet, another as an engineer, a third as a miner, etc. Thus, constancy of objective perception is one of the major assumptions of testing.

Another assumption relating to testing is that any personal or individual characteristic is normally distributed within a given population. Obviously, the population must consist of a large enough number of individuals to constitute a relevant sample of individuals. This means that characteristics such as height, weight, intelligence, etc., are assumed to be normally distributed throughout the total human population. These observations initially developed in the physical sciences have been applied to measurement theory in the question of testing characteristics, whether they be physical, mental, or personality traits.

Still another assumption which is made in testing relates to the question of intervening variables. In modern psychological learning theory, behavioral events have been identified in terms of stimulus situations, intervening variables, and responses. The stimulus situation is considered to be that event, act, or phenomenon which causes a chain of events to occur within the individual organism. The response behavior is interpreted as the terminal act of the stimulus as it proceeds through the intervening variables to the external observable forum as a response. Psychologists do not have a comprehensive explanation for the nature of the intervening variables at this time. However, it is apparent that the emotional need system of individuals, their patterns of learned behavior, the cultural context, their intelligence, aptitude, and past behavior, together with the physiological state of the organism, all alter and modify the nature of the response event.

Testing, then, is a scientific procedure based on the assumptions of constancy of perception, normal distribution of physical and mental phenomena, and the stimulus-response paradigm. Testing is one particular means of assessment and evaluation. Evaluation is a much broader concept and includes a variety of other methods such as personal observation, the report of others, etc. Testing is characterized by two specific factors: 1) objectivity and 2) standardization. This means that ordinarily a test is related to specific occurrences in time and space, consists of a set of tasks which are judged uniform for all individuals tested, and must be administered and scored in a specific way. Evaluation, on the other hand, can extend over an indefinite period of time, can be based on various criteria of excellence or poor behavior, and can include a variety of other forms of observation.

The key words in testing are objectivity and standardization. Even teacher-made tests used in the classroom are attempts to provide some degree of objective assessment, even though usually no effort is made to standardize such instruments. In order to construct a valid test, *i.e.*, one which objectively provides a basis for evaluation of certain defined characteristics, it is necessary to proceed systematically through a number of steps. These steps include the assembly of a pool of legitimate tasks or stimulus events which are characteristic of the trait or phenomenon to be measured, the systematic testing of these tasks or events on representative populations, the elimination of inappropriate items, and the construction of what are called norms. Without norms, test scores cannot be interpreted. Norms are based on the average performance of representative groups of individuals, and their chief purpose is to show to the test interpreter or test scorer the relative position of individuals in relationship to the total group. Thus, for example, through testing and preliminary experimental studies, one can learn what is "normal" for a nine year old child to know. *However,* the judgment of what is normal for a nine year old child depends on the careful step-by-step procedure detailed above in standardization. Unless the test construction procedure is carefully worked out, the standardization will be inaccurate, the norms misleading, and individual test scores erroneous.

Furthermore, even when test instruments are carefully standardized there is always what is called a standard error of measurement. This means that there is a built-in error of measurement in any test. Conditions which are not susceptible to control, such as the personal feelings of the child, the conditions of the testing situation, or actual errors in scoring and interpretation, result in this error of measurement. For example, the 1960 revision of the Stanford-Binet Intelligence Scale has an error of measurement of approximately 5 I.Q. points. This means that a child who obtains an I.Q. of 95 could have a true I.Q. falling anywhere between 90 and 100. Similar problems exist in other tests such as achievement tests and may be even greater in personality tests.

The standard error of measurement also relates to another factor, *i.e.*, what is called regression towards the mean. This simply means that one testing result may be either low or high. On another testing of the same instrument children who scored low for personal reasons or poor testing circumstances may tend to obtain a higher score. Likewise high scoring children may obtain a lower score. Sometimes people just guess more accurately than at other times. So likewise, they may feel more like taking the test and put more effort and motivation into it. In any event, the standard error of measurement together with the concept of regression towards the mean are both factors which relate to the objectivity of the testing instrument and above all to the confidence which should be placed in test scores.

Still another problem of the objective and standardized test is the fact that sometimes individuals may miss an identical number of items on a test and come up with a similar score, but they are not identical from the point of view of individual differences. Since test scores and norms based on test scores often are concerned with the absolute number of items answered correctly or falsely, two individuals who miss different specific items may still obtain the same test score.

All of these problems accent the difficulties which exist in relationship to careful test construction and standardization. They are often ignored in test interpretation by counselors and others. Testing is simply an objectivized method of arriving at decisions about the characteristics of individuals and groups. Its essential characteristic therefore is related to its value as an objective method of decision-making. The characteristics of a given population can be more adequately assessed on the basis of an objective and standardized test instrument than by any other known means. However, there are limitations to the interpretation of these results, limitations which relate not only to the assumptions made about testing theory itself, but about the construction of the scales, the items included, the population tested, the preliminary studies, and a whole host of factors relating to the testing situation itself. As a result, though testing provides an objective basis for assessment and evaluation of group characteristics, *it is always most valid for groups* and *least valid for individuals*. Thus, we can be more sure of describing *groups* of individuals in terms of test-derived scores and characteristics than we can in describing *an individual* within that group. The best test devised can only give us some very qualified information about individuals, and this qualified information is dependent on many possible sources of error. *Therefore test results should be used by professionals as one possible objective method of improving the decision-making process regarding individuals.* The writer knows of no test which administered one time to an individual should be used as an absolute measure of that person's intelligence, personality, interests or other characteristics.

The functions of testing are related to the evaluation of group characteristics. The primary purpose of testing is to determine the characteristics of large groups of individuals and to determine how specific individuals compare with these reference groups. However, tests are also used to improve the judgment and decision-making process for other organizations or groups in our culture. Implicit in this use of testing is the notion of prediction. The common sense basis of our judgment process is founded on the notion of prediction. Society could not exist without the formation and sustaining of predictive patterns of behavior. By predictive patterns of behavior in individuals is meant a stable, organized manner of responding to systematic stimuli. This means simply that any form of culture, technological or not, depends for its survival upon organized and consistent patterns of behavior. Individuals learn what are the characteristic and typical responses to love, fear, excitement, and other kinds of stimuli. These characteristics are different, depending on the level and nature of the culture and the sophistication of response repertories developed by the culture. They are transmitted through education and the total nurturance pattern of the culture. Thus, testing as a peculiar modern method for objective assessment of characteristics has assumed a very important function as a means of prediction of success or failure in our society. For example, it is ordinarily assumed that the best guarantee of future achievement is related to past and present achievement. Similar assumptions are made about the results of personality adjustment, intellectual functioning, etc. However, the prediction of individual behavior from test variables in fraught with difficulties chiefly because prediction is a kind of secondary by-product of testing rather than the primary goal implicit in testing theory. Typical examples of prediction in testing are the equations developed between test results obtained in an achievement type test in high school and grade-point average in college. Here the total group of test scores is related to a total group of grade point averages. The prediction is made on the basis of the ordering of the first set of scores (predictor variables) to the second set of scores (criterion variables). But individual prediction, even based on a special method called an expectancy table, is difficult to arrive at. The best that can be said regarding any individual is that his pattern of scores (if they are truly representative of his ability) provides an estimate of a specific kind of grade-point average within a collegiate setting.

This problem of prediction then relates to another question which is far from resolved in testing. That question concerns the matter of criteria. A criterion is considered to be an external measure which relates to some kind of effective behavior. In the college prediction studies mentioned above, the criterion was grade-point average. This is a straightforward kind of mathematical index which can easily serve as a criterion in the assessment of collegiate behavior. However, many authorities in this field recognize how inadequate grade-point average is as a true measurement of achievement in college. It has these advantages: 1) nearly all professors recognize the importance of grades; and 2) it is easily computed and plugged into the analysis of the relationship between predictor variables (test scores obtained earlier in this case) and criterion variables. But the grade-point average does not measure the qualities of a collegiate education in terms of creativity, inter-personal relationships, aspiration levels, motivation, and a host of other factors. It will not tell us why a low-achieving high school student may turn out to be a highly productive and creative individual by dint of hard work. Rather, it favors the high achieving youngster who most likely will continue to achieve.

The criterion problem remains one of the central problems of testing. A criterion must relate to the question of what constitutes effective human behavior in a given situation or circumstance. This is the paramount and inescapable fact. Not only is this true for the collegiate setting, but it is true for the broader contexts of life. The logic of this is evident when one considers for a moment the fact that testing is a means of assessment of human behavior. But if testing is to be used as a means of prediction or, at the very least, of improving judgment about individuals, what is the relationship between test scores and criteria of effective human behavior? These questions must be answered when test scores are used in relationship to decision-making about the future. Are the scores related to effective criteria? Or have the test scores themselves become the criteria? This is an important point which has been too long ignored by test users. *Test scores should not be considered as criteria of effective human behavior.* Test scores may be judged, under proper circumstances, to relate to criteria of behavior, but they are not the criteria themselves.

In an article about the criterion problem, Astin (1965) pointed out that a criterion is essentially ecological in nature and is not contingent upon a relationship to any antecedent variable.

> In contrast to a purely psychological construct or trait, a criterion variable usually refers to a relationship between the person and his environment. It is, in fact, difficult to speak of 'standards' of performance or of behavior as being 'desirable' without also defining the social context in which the behavior occurs.

Astin indicts the efforts of those who would set about creating a testing instrument, standardizing it, and then assuming that the test score is the criterion. He points out that one of the most common misconceptions about criteria is that they can be "validated" either through inter-correlation procedures or factor analysis.

Obviously, the problem of determining what constitutes effective human behavior is tied up with epistemological and axiological problems. There is a wide range of philosophical speculation concerning what constitutes the "good life," what hierarchies of certitude to accept, and the ordering of personal values. Though all of this philosophical inquiry is relevant to the individual in its intentionalistic or phenomenological locus, the external criterion of his behavior is judged in the societal or cultural context. Thus, the common element of man's humanity is that he lives, breathes, and behaves in a cultural setting. Culture judges effective human behavior because culture controls patterning and, either subtly or bluntly, provides the criterion reinforcement for specific kinds of social behavior.

Because of the importance of the criterion variable in testing and the relationship of testing to the measurement of behavior, the balance of this chapter will explore the nature of culture, assessment in its cultural perspective, and the social consequences of testing as a cultural means of evaluation, prediction, and control.

The Nature of Culture

Man lives in a social environment. He is constantly being affected by the culture in which he lives. This process begins at birth and continues throughout life. By culture is meant not that popular understanding of the term as it relates to girls' "finishing schools" or using the proper fork at a banquet table, but rather the sum total of man's learned behavior in a social environment. Thus any aspect of our day-to-day behavior is included under this concept of culture. Culture used in this manner refers to that which is tangible, such as automobiles, toothbrushes, skyscrapers, and astronauts' capsules. It also refers to intangible behavior and includes wishes, hopes, fears, and ways of thinking. Culture so used includes the optimism of Americans, as well as the fears of Russia that she will be attacked by encircling nations. It comprises the hopes of the young African nations that they can develop a technological civilization.

There are varying attitudes towards culture. One is that culture is an absolute entity, seen as a huge, super-organic, all-enveloping constellation of controls which determines everything about a particular society (Bidley, 1947). In this view, culture becomes a sort of self-generating, autonomous force which evolves according to fixed laws. It determines all behavior absolutely. As a corollary, the only possible way of understanding any individual's behavior is by understanding his society. Another point of view regarding culture is a more humanistic one. Christopher Dawson (1934) has expressed the view that culture is a spiritual community which owes its unity to common beliefs and a common attitude towards life. A less dichotomous position towards culture is taken by Kluckhohn (1945). He sees culture as a series of historically created patterns serving as potential guides for human conduct. This view mediates between the two extreme views in that a determinism is recognized, but it is not absolute. The customs of a group may, at times, be abrogated under some circumstances. No one must absolutely follow the regulations of his culture. However, if an individual wills to remain within the social setting, he wills the means to that end unless he wishes to suffer from exclusion.

Since all of us grow up in one culture or the other, we learn cultural behavior by a process of imitation and shaping which is, for the most part, unconscious. We behave in certain ways without really being aware that we are behaving in conformity with our culture. This process of "enculturation" continues until an individual is unmistakably a Frenchman, an American, or a bushman. It is precisely this subliminal learning of a culture that makes for so many amusing and tragic reactions when one thoroughly "enculturated" person visits another culture. This accounts for amused reactions to an African tribal dance, shock over different sexual customs, and horror over the drinking habits of Europeans. We learn our culture by living it. We do not inherit culture through our genes, as we inherit a tendency towards blue eyes or blond hair.

Social behavior is learned in specific ways. One major determinant is the systematic process of shaping human behavior through selective reinforcement procedures. The reward of parental or social peers in response to appropriate behavior reinforces this behavior. Secondly, the individual's perception of his reality is shaped through imitation, modeling, play activities, and the development of roles. In the earlier cultural systems, the existence of an elaborate kinship system and the sanctioning of certain customs presented a model of behavior which was transmitted to children. Thus, boys learned to identify with certain kinds of behaviors by watching the males of the tribes. They may have envied their status and looked forward to this status. They knew that they had to conform to group procedures in hunting and other matters. Deviation could expose both them and the group to the most dire consequences.

Then, as in the present, much of our early development is structured along the directions of those command phrases which our parents and others are constantly using to shape our behavior. As children, we are dependent creatures. We did not choose to be born, nor do we choose when we shall eat or sleep, or what clothes we shall wear, or when we may play, sit, read, or study. The reactions to this process of environmental controls have been identified clinically. Some of us apparently internalize the conflicting expectations of society and our needs. Others become aggressive and strike back in either covert or overt ways at the very controls which force us to behave in certain ways. Often the early control system lasts into later life. We are told as children to eat so that we may grow up strong like daddy. And so we unconsciously equate food with strength and power and continue to overeat well into our maturity. Early explorations of sexual organs often result in severe indictments with fears of loss of love, sanity, or threat of ill health. In our emotional life, dirt, black, evil, sin, and sex often become one end of a continuum, whereas cleanliness, white, virtue, and repression become the other end.

Thus the criterion of effective human behavior emerges as conformity to cultural expectations. We learn that if we are to obtain approval of ourselves we must learn to make certain kinds of responses to certain kinds of social expectations or stimuli. Through the process of operant conditioning, we try out alternate courses of action in our behavior repertory. These successive approximations are judged against the criterion of peer and superior responses. Ultimately, the laws and customs of our society join themselves to peers and superiors. From our simple learning to the more complex procedures of social intercourse we learn both how to generalize our behavior approximations and to make discriminatory judgments about special circumstances. Patterns are built up. These patterns are called habits, and as the habits become more firmly imbedded in our response repertory they subtly alter and direct the nature of our perception. The mind is structured in its mode of learning and perceiving by its physiological organization as well as social reinforcement. If the rationale of Berlyne (1960) and Taylor (1962) is correct, the brain-stem reticular activating system which spreads its fibres throughout the brain-stem and into the thalamus plays a vital part in both learning and perception. For it would appear that this system first relays impulses from any sense receptor to any part of the cortex and that later cortical differentiations appear through a process of conditioned responses. It would appear that the child's early perceptual responses are gradually tied down (neurologically speaking) by the social and personal reinforcers of such early object relations as the mother's smile, her approving caressing, etc.

Culture or man's social response to living in groups would appear to be the chief reinforcer or patterner of individual social behavior. Effective human behavior would seem to be contextual to the culture and expressed by patterns of stable predictable behavior which is in essential agreement with the expectations of a given cultural milieu.

Assessment and its Cultural Perspective

From the puberty rites of the upper Paleolithic period to present day forms of objective testing, evaluation has played an important part in cultural control. Evaluation as a means of intellectual and personality assessment plays a central role in the transmission of those forms of behavior deemed essential to the survival of a culture. It is the way in which a given society makes sure that individuals promoted to certain roles are indeed ready and capable of assuming those roles. Man has always felt the need of defining certain characteristics which were needed for successful functioning. Conforming behavior in a social setting became the first major criterion for this assessment. Certain present or past characteristics were deemed to be predictors of future congruence to the criterion. Though the early predictors were variously assessed in terms of manliness, hunting prowess, knowledge of sexual mores, and recognition of authority, they emerged in early societies as meaningful dimensions of evaluation or assessment. The more specific criteria of effective human conduct were basically related to stable predictable patterns of behavior which were deemed consonant with the survival of the group. Thus stable predictable behavior was invested in a routine and sanctioned by ritual practices. Eventually certain kinds of behavior developed into powerful means of education. Early man with his own trial-and-error method found that certain characteristics which were observable or testable were reliable predictors of stable group behavior.

In order to insure the criteria of effective and predictable human behavior, a number of cultural mechanisms of control emerged. These mechanisms of control had as their goal the collective security of the group. They are identifiable as the family, customs, law, chieftains, religious beliefs and leaders, and education. To early man they represented the concrete framework which was a most important one, for it was through the process of education, whether formal or informal, that the cultural heritage was transmitted and the survival of the group insured.

The earliest form of assessment or evaluation was global in nature. Though no attempt was made to separate intellectual functioning from personality, the behavior patterns of the individual were subjected to the criterion of group collective security. The behavior repertory of the individual was examined and scrutinized by those who were in a position of authority to determine whether there were identifiable patterns of predictable and stable behavior. The early leaders of men were empirical psychologists. Homer and the Bible provide examples of the psychological wisdom of early men. Ulysses on one occasion, not wishing to go to war, pretended to be mad. He began to plow a field sowing salt. One of his friends placed his young son directly in front of the plow and Ulysses turned aside, showing indeed that he was not mad and could not escape fulfilling his promises. The Bible itself is filled with descriptions of how behavior was assessed. In the account of Genesis, Adam hid himself and God is portrayed as being aware that something was wrong because of this change in behavior. Likewise, in one of the early tribal wars the men of Gilead found a way to distinguish between friendly and unfriendly groups. They asked suspects to pronounce the word Shibboleth; if they could not pronounce it correctly, they were judged to be enemies.

The oral examination plus prescribed feats of courage served as a predictor of effective behavior among early men. Later on, as formal education developed, the degree of memory recall and conformity to school expectations also became a part of the evaluation procedure. Whether observation was used alone or as part of a selective questioning procedure, this technique possessed power functions for prediction in the sense that it provided certain behavioral cues which could be detected and identified even in the absence of a logical rationale to explain the procedure.

It was not long before a theoretical framework was joined to the observation procedure. Plato in his hierarchy of society demarcated certain kinds of behavior expected of various levels of society. He expected the philosopher-rulers to manifest verbal ability and intellectual wisdom, the soldiers and warriors to evince courage and manliness, and the vast masses to be concerned only with bodily functions. Hippocrates discerned differences in men's constitutional make-up, suggesting that all individuals fell into the categories of phlegmatic, choleric, sanguine, or melancholic. The oral examination, used either by itself or in conjunction with a philosophical position, emerged as an important part of the medieval university where a student was not compelled to attend any number of regular lectures. The essential burden of evaluation or assessment in medieval education was placed on an elaborate variation of the oral interview in which a candidate for a degree was examined by a group of university "masters" before his peers. This took the form of defending a thesis in which the full complement of the young scholar's abilities was brought to bear during the process of presenting an argument and defending it against the attacks of his superiors and peers. The advantage of this type of assessment of behavior, from the evaluation point of view, was that it provided not only some index of the personal knowledge of the candidate, but also some idea as to how well a given individual could think on his feet, providing opposing arguments to the charges made against his thesis and dealing with the general stress of the situation. This form of oral examination is still with us in the modern university, where it is used extensively both in foreign and American institutions to determine competency of master's and doctoral candidates.

The use of personal observation and interviewing has always been structured by the needs of the cultural group. These needs provide the point of view or the frame of reference. Even as in early cultures the assessment of men related to personal skills and prowess in hunting and warfare, so later in medieval times monks were scrutinized to determine whether they possessed the kinds of characteristics needed in the monastic life. For example, Ignatius Loyola and his followers developed systematic means for assessing the spiritual life of Jesuits and evaluating the characteristics of their neophytes. But in all of these periods, the generalized observation emerges that means for the assessment of men were always directed by the frame of reference relating to survival of the group. Deviation has always been considered dangerous because it indicates divergent thinking, which cannot be related to predictable, stable patterns of behavior.

With the nineteenth century further developments took place in the assessment of behavior. An extension of the oral examination was developed in an essay examination. Used extensively in the developing universities of the 19th century, it still remains as one means of evaluating student ability in a more global manner. A given topic is provided for discussion, evaluation, comparison, and other purposes. The student is expected to marshall his whole knowledge of the subject and his ability to organize concepts in the answer he writes.

The development of more quantitative methods in assessing human behavior had to wait until the nineteenth century for its beginnings. During the 19th century, methods of measurement used in the physical and biological sciences were gradually introduced into the study of human behavior. This approach was sparked by a desire to become more objective in the analysis of human behavior. Derived in part from the accelerated studies in physiology of Muller, Helmholtz, Maudsley, and others, the general contention was that the key to the understanding of human behavior was to be found in an understanding of the nature of the biological organism and the collection of measurement data regarding reflexes, perception, stature, and the sensory avenues. In part also, the movement was augmented by the study of Darwin's theory of natural selection concept. This approach lent credence to the notion that heredity endowed various men with superior intelligences and was a capacity fixed once and for all by genetic inheritance. Galton (1896) in a study of genius found that most of the significant contributions of great men in Britain were confined to a number of families. He failed to recognize the privileged status of these families in terms of cultural enrichment. But he did pursue the study of individual differences, devising many tests of simple sensory and motor functions to measure reaction time, etc. Further, he provided the statistical basis for the comparison of groups and specific behaviors.

Binet and Simon, charged with the task of developing an objective type measurement instrument in the area of intelligence, criticized Galton's studies as being too narrowly physiological in nature. They were concerned with the two principal problems of assessment in differential psychology: 1) to determine the nature and extent of individual differences, and 2) to discover the interrelationships of mental processes within the individual. With the measurement data which Binet and Simon obtained, a variety of rapid developments took place. Cattell, a student of Galton, coined the term mental test in 1890. Goddard translated the Binet scale into English in 1908 and used it in the Vineland Training School. In his studies of the Kallikak family, he arrived at the notion that the measurements were indeed providing an assessment of hereditary differences. Stern, the German psychologist, provided a rationale for the testing results on the basis of mental age and chronological age. Terman in 1946 revised the earlier instrument and popularized its usage.

In the area of objective mass testing, the work of J. M. Rice in the United States seems to have made one of the first attempts to use the methods which have developed into objective testing. In the last decade of the nineteenth century, he devised a spelling test of 50 words and learned that children in one school could spell as well with only fifteen minutes a day for eight years as those who had spent thirty minutes a day for eight years (Ayers, 1918).

Though the presentation of these results brought on Rice almost unlimited attack from educational circles, who denounced his findings as foolish, reprehensible, and from every point of view indefensible, little by little thoughtful men began to appreciate the value of what Dr. Rice had demonstrated. Thorndike developed a test for measurement of handwriting in 1909, measurement clinics sprung up throughout the country, and the development of mass testing through objective techniques was under way. From the early tests relating to the quality of handwriting and arithmetic knowledge a variety of techniques were developed which made it possible to use true-false categories, multiple-choice alternatives, matching, and other procedures. During the first World War, the development of the Army Alpha series and the Otis tests of intelligence demonstrated that the objective test was here to stay. Hundreds of tests were soon developed, and in more recent years these tests have moved from single scores to multiple scores and dimensions. Not only have thousands of tests been standardized by scientific procedures, but nearly every school teacher now uses objective tests to determine how well learning is going in his class.

Since the enactment of the 1958 National Defense Education Act with its concern about able students, funds have been provided for large-scale testing programs in secondary schools to identify students with outstanding aptitudes and abilities. The states acted to establish state-wide testing programs. Large scale testing programs were supported by research and private foundations, and nearly every college and university has adopted some testing program to evaluate or screen applicants for admission. The development of the large-scale testing programs such as the College Entrance Examination Board, the American College Testing Program, and the National Merit Scholarship program has become an accepted part of evaluation in modern American education.

Accompanying the expansion of testing programs, a new technological development in the use of scoring machines and computers has made the analysis of data easy and economical to obtain. Further, complex mathematical calculations can be obtained in a matter of minutes on thousands of cases. In today's world a brief article in a journal can report a study in which 127,211 students were tested on a battery of instruments composed of 52 student "input" variables (Astin, 1964b). Such a gigantic task would have been impossible twenty years ago. Turing (in Harcleroad, 1964) stated in 1950 that within fifty years time it should be possible to program computers with a storage capacity of about 10^9 and for these computers to be able to outwit a human being in about five minutes. Computers today are being used in every phase of government, business, automobile control for freeways, and even in biblical studies. A revolution in the processing, flow, and control of information is in the making. In June, 1964, Congressman Puscinski proposed a bill (H. R. 1964) to establish a "National Research Data Processing and Information Retrieval Center" whereby university libraries, industrial laboratories, and other sources of information could be linked in a tremendous nerve center.

Even more fantastic uses of computers are now being envisaged. One such project is attempting to devise ways and means for connecting many small sub-stations to the console of a large computer, so that immediate access can be had by many individuals to the large computer. Another is the large scale use being made of scanners in industry to facilitate reading or sending bills. At present Sperry-Rand has compressed a big Univac computer into a six inch box through the use of transistorized circuits. "Scientists have constructed miniaturized circuits so small that 20,000 of them, each doing the work of an ordinary radio tube, could be placed on a postage stamp" (Turing). Wiener, the founder of cybernetics, conjectured that in the next decade or so computer memories will be developed that have elements akin to genes, and input and output problems will be solved by light of specific molecular spectra. Southard (in Harcleroad, 1964) writes:

> As long ago as May, 1960, a panel of 'experts' at the Western Joint Computer Conference in San Francisco predicted that within ten years it would be possible to 'walk into a computer store' and, for the price of a new automobile, walk out with a computer the size of a golf ball or maybe as large as a grapefruit. This computer would have the capacity of IBM's 7030 (Stretch), a computer with up to 262,000 sixty-four bit words of storage and a 1.5 microsecond add time and would have the 'intelligence' of a fresh baccalaureate degree holder from college.

The fantastic developments in computer technology and data processing illustrate dramatically the new dimensions of assessment procedures. It is possible to compare individuals or groups of individuals with large samples and norms developed from these large samples. But though the procedures have become exceedingly advanced, it is quite apparent that testing in this setting has moved away from the original intent of assessment procedures. The early procedures were related to making judgments about the predicted success or failure of an individual within a specific cultural setting. The present direction of testing, despite its technical and methodological excellence, subtly introduces a new criterion of excellence, i.e., comparison with the average. Explicitly or implicitly, the test score becomes a criterion in itself rather than a means to an end. The mathematical symbol becomes all too often the criterion of expected performance without any real reference to the behavioral phenomena needed for success in the cultural setting.

Changing Mechanisms of Cultural Control

One of the inevitable consequences of harnessing more and more energy through technology is change in the patterns of a given civilization. The industrial revolution provides one example of this fact and our present culture exemplifies another. With changes in our technology have come profound changes in the basic anchors of society. Man's earliest sociology of groups held that certain stable patterns of behavior were necessary to maintain the security of the group, engage in collective food-gathering, and provide for mutual protection. The extended family, customs, law, ethics, religion, priesthood, chieftains, police functions, and education all seem to have developed as man's unique response to his environment. The mechanisms of control which evolved possessed a basic stabilizing effect on society. This was done by creating a psychological sense of security through a degree of predictability of behavior. In terms of learning theory, these control mechanisms were the great social reinforcers which developed in every member of the society a repertoire of appropriate responses. *In a very real sense, then, cultural mechanisms of control had as their goal and function the evaluation, prediction, and control of behavioral phenomena.* Through measured experience as a criterion, man obtained in a pre-scientific manner that which he has attempted to obtain in more recent ages through science.

These controls, however, were chiefly imposed on man from without. The individual had little choice but to conform to existing control mechanisms. They were specifically attached to the group, culture, or nation and automatically provided answers regarding what was right and what was wrong, what was accepted and what was not. If man did not know himself the answers to his persistent questions, he could find out by asking the "authorities." The bases of these controls were centered in the strong position of the family and the familial culture. The basic position was one of ethnocentrism or a conviction that one's own group was superior to all others, or at least most others. Another factor bolstering this control was the fact that the family was often anchored to the land and dependent on an agrarian economy. Later on, a common religious heritage derived from nationalistic origin also became a common control mechanism.

Today the characteristics of American culture have changed radically. A 1958 survey showed that one out of five Americans moved geographically within that year. Our culture is highly technological, with demands for large populations of technicians, highly skilled workmen, and pools of brain power. Great complexes of industrial and technological "know-how" have been amassed in strategic areas of the nation. The ever-increasing utilization of energy forms through technology has demanded a highly mobile nation. As a result, the typical control mechanisms of the past have weakened, giving rise to the charge by many that there is a sense of cultural "ennui" or "drift in values."

The effects of our cultural mobility have been many and varied. The traditional anchors of the land, a religion based on the land such as in the old European tradition of "whose land, his religion" (*Cuius regio, ejus religio*), and a family of assured social status have all but disappeared in modern American life. Mobility today means that in most instances the family exists alone in a strange area. Very seldom do uncles, aunts, cousins, grandparents and others reside next door or even in the same area. Mobility means that the significance of property as a psychological anchor and root has been changed. Banks indicate that the average length of occupancy of a house with a twenty-five year mortgage is seven years. Changes in sex roles have resulted so that women are coming to marriage not with feather beds, cooking ability, and canning prowess, but with professional skills in such fields as teaching, nursing, or secretarial work. Mobility has resulted in changing patterns of housing, such as are seen in the vast suburban developments where relatively homogeneous groupings are imposed by qualifying salary criteria and contracting agreements. Changes in the strength of institutional religion have also occurred. It is a well known fact that a large part of our population changes its religious affiliation either by marriage or personal preference.

Methods of child-rearing have also changed with accent on more permissive patterns of child-rearing. From more direct controls the family has learned to rely on more indirect ones. Boys get less punishment and girls less indulgence and protectiveness. Though girls are possibly less debilitated by parental affection and power, boys find it more difficult to identify clear roles to envy or emulate. The end result may be that the procedures themselves are less effective in the development of leadership and responsibility in children. Miller and Swanson (1958) have interpreted these results as an indication that America is moving towards a bureaucratic society that emphasizes "getting along rather than getting ahead."

It is furthermore apparent that the economic value of a college education is recognized by most youth. While opportunities for college attendance are being made greater, there is also a continued effort on the part of institutions of higher learning to become more and more selective in admissions. As a result, students even in the elementary school are beginning to feel the pressure to achieve at all costs.

To all of these changes must be added the continual crisis orientation of modern political developments, with the need for competitive
achievement in the areas of space satellites, moon probes and atomic
defense arsenals. The international scene for the past twenty years
has been one of continued peaks of anxiety about global destruction
and warfare. There is a strong suspicion on the part of many that our
very economic welfare hinges on continued huge expenditures for
military preparedness. Federal programs, often in response to international demands or conditions, have affected large segments of our
population through educational programs and defense contract spending. Meanwhile, within the United States itself, riots and demon-
strations have marked the difficult struggle of the Negro citizen to
overcome the traditional restrictions of older ethnocentric cultural
defenses.

In response to these changes a period of disorganization has been
"divined" by some and "felt" by many. Efforts have been made to
swing the United States back into a conservative frame of reference.
The allegations have been made that present trends are "socialistic,"
with the implications being that this is the same as "communistic."
Others have attacked the role of the federal government in American
life. But those who attack federal subsidies do not want these subsidies removed, and those who decry federal spending do not wish
military defenses and bases that employ thousands reduced. The
entire picture is one of great confusion about the goals and values of
American life. The same situation exists in education where parents
wish their children to receive a well-rounded education, but in depth!
They wish them to be intellectual but still "adjusted" to group pressures and codes. Though there are many causes for our present state
of cultural disorganization, one explanation of these national anxieties
is that because of advanced technological development, a partial disintegration has taken place in our externalized control mechanisms.
The toleration of multiple value systems, the emphasis on democratic
processes of decision-making, despite the fact that group decisions may
be wrong, and the search for meaning in all the facets of advanced
research have resulted in much unrest, both physical and mental, on
the part of individuals and groups. The cultural anchors of man's
psychological security have been uprooted, and man's challenge to the
alternative of being controlled from external sources has resulted in
the unparalleled task of developing controls from within. Essentially,
man's social and psychological orientation to cultural controls has not
kept pace with the changes which are occurring all too rapidly in the
dimensions of technological change.

New Mechanisms of Cultural Control

The partial disintegration of some of the older external control mechanisms and the development of a new technology have resulted in some new devices which have all of the trappings of control mechanisms. Mass media of communication and large scale testing programs are two of these devices. They have this in common with traditional mechanisms of control, in that they have come to represent means for bringing about a certain amount of unanticipated stability and cohesion in our society. Boskoff (1959) has suggested that television and other mass media of communication do this by: 1) scattering or diversion of audience attention; 2) re-focusing of existing tensions and their reduction by the semblance of an expanding scale through myriad contacts with distant places and personages; 3) the illusion of modernity and the appeal to the latest which is really new as a criterion of value; 4) providing a sense of confidence in a remote authority derived from the pronouncements of official cultural idols and heroes; and 5) providing an important element of ritual regularity and predictability vested in such expected symbols as the regular T.V. program, the daily newspaper, and the weekly magazine. It is interesting to ponder the fact that though we may move from state to state, change jobs, and find ourselves in situations where we must adapt to new roles, we can always find one element of national stability in the Jackie Gleason show, the Perry Como show, or the Huntley-Brinkley report.

Testing as a means of educational evaluation has also emerged as a cultural control mechanism. More and more in our society education has become important as a means to economic success. As the school has assumed more of the original functions of home and church, testing has also become more prominent. From the readiness tests taken in kindergarten to the Graduate Record Examination, students take hundreds and even thousands of standardized, individual, and teacher-made tests. Education, too, is one cultural mechanism which has increased in its importance. Though people may move, there are always schools, and the tests, though different, are always there. For testing has come to represent one major criterion of personal evaluation which can operate effectively within a highly mobile and technological culture. As with television, testing has come to represent a criterion of evaluation and excellence which effects a measure of stability and cohesion in the educational process. It is vested in an ultimate authority, the scientific process. And it certainly has an element of ritual regularity because as every student knows, when one testing is over, another will soon begin. Students, high schools, institutions of higher learning, and the community at large have come to accept testing as an inevitable part of education.

These two new mechanisms of control present both some assets and liabilities. In the plus column one can see all of the learning possibilities which are in television and the other media of communication. Lectures can be taped, whole courses can be given via television. Excellent programs can be presented to masses of people, providing them with a cultural richness never before possible. And then, let us concede the fact, who can doubt the very real psychological relaxation that television provides by way of escape from the hum-drum day-to-day existence, the pressures of achievement and status, and the accelerated heartbeat of the freeway traffic! So it is with testing. The measurement of the educational product is a means to self-direction and curriculum change for the school and the individual — if used, and used correctly. Moreover, the objective measurement of achievement is certainly a good one in itself. Furthermore, the procedure of testing is an important link in the discovery of new scientific information not only about the content aspect of education but about the process of learning itself.

But despite some of the advantages of television and testing, there are hazards also. Consider the effects of a steady diet of aggression and hostility in television viewing on the behavior of children. Bandura and his associates (1963) have demonstrated that children watching an aggressive form of behavior in a film show considerable aggressive behavior afterwards. This was found in comparison with children watching models who displayed inhibited and nonaggressive behavior. There are frequent reports of how acts of violence or robberies have been conceived through the observation of plots on television.[3] Obviously, one way to control this situation is to have governmental control of the mass media. Since this solution or other similar ones is unacceptable to most individuals, the alternative is to exercise individual control enforcing certain family criteria of excellence.

In a similar vein, testing too has tended to become a standard unto itself. Though here again governmental control would be unwise, it is most likely that the testing devices have tended to control the course of education rather than the other way around. Moreover, test scores have tended to be regarded as something akin to absolutes and, therefore, inviolate. Controls need to be established which are consonant with the educational objectives of our institutions.

---

[3] For example the San Francisco Examiner (November 13, 1964) related how a group of teen age children had developed a series of robberies netting them over $5,000.00 on the basis of a formula presented in a television program.

The Social Impact of Testing

The question of social consequences of testing recalls two historical illustrations drawn from the ancient civilizations of China and Rome. Dubois in an interesting presentation (1964) has noted that test makers establish goals for individuals and influence the shape of social institutions. He has recalled that imperial China had a tradition of using systematic tests for over 3000 years, a fact which has been largely ignored by contemporary psychometricians. China established a kind of civil service examination about 1115 B.C. This system continued with slight modifications until 1905. The system was based on the notion that a hereditary aristocracy was not the best way to perpetuate sound government. As a result appointments to both local and regional control positions were based on a series of very severe examinations. Though some testing seems to have existed as early as 2200 B.C., there is a clear record of formal examinations in the Chan dynasty (1115 B.C.). Sample tests were used requiring proficiency in the five basic arts — music, archery, horsemanship, writing, and arithmetic. Knowledge of a sixth area, skill in the rites and ceremonies of public life, was also required. Subsequently, with the introduction of Confucianism certain moral standards were also required, and familiarity with the geography of the empire, civil law, military matters, agriculture, and the administration of revenue were items added to the comprehensive testing.

The tests were administered at three levels. Any individual could apply to take the test in his district capitol. If he did well, he would be permitted to take another battery of tests at the provincial capitol. Usually some 20 or so would be picked out to attend the testing sessions at the provincial capitol which took place each third year under the supervision of scholars sent from Peking. A handful of scholars were then picked from the provincial examinations and registered in the national competition. If a scholar were successful in the national competition he was easily given access to the political and governmental positions available in the empire. Meanwhile provincial and district posts were available to those who had passed the examinations at the other levels.

Dubois mentions that these examinations were direct attempts at objective assessment of individual differences. The circumstances surrounding the testing situation were carefully controlled. The candidates' names were carefully concealed and examinations were often read by two or more independent examiners who handed their sealed evaluations to a third examiner, who reconciled any differences. Scores were obtained on the basis of rank order. As Dubois (1966) states:

In this year 1964 when psychological tests are being used more and more extensively at critical points in the careers of all our citizens, we will do well to consider their effects on individuals, on specific institutions, and on society. The long Chinese experience is a pertinent case history. It is a plausible hypothesis that much of the great strength of the Chinese empire came from the intellectual vigor of men who were bright enough to compete in examinations requiring the writing of poems and 'eight-legged essays.'

Moreover, it is important to recognize that political and financial rewards were attached to success in these examinations. A system of rewards based on achievement reinforced the aspirations of budding scholars to compete for a place of recognized stature within the empire. Further, many western nations have studied these examinations and have incorporated some elements into their national civil service examinations. It seems to have influenced in one way or another both the French and British civil service systems, as well as that developed in the United States.

This historical example contrasts favorably with another historical example, i.e., the civil service system of the Roman Empire. Under Augustus an extensive civil service system was established. For many years this civil service system tended to build up an independent middle class group in the cities and provinces of the empire. The system promoted local individuals to minor positions of importance. This wise system tended to build local support for the empire, particularly since it was not directly tied to the raising of local revenues for state use. Subsequently, however, the system became more and more hereditary as the empire felt the problems of debased currency, population loss, poor communications, and invasions. The military tended to dominate all decisions, and the original impetus of the system was lost. No one wished to be a civil servant because local leaders were held responsible for more and more tax collection. Their estates and lands were forfeited if they could not meet these regular and extraordinary levies for funds.

These two historical examples point out some of the advantages to testing procedures. The attempt at objectivity, the access to high position based on achievement and ability, and the reliance on a set of quasi-standardized responses all point to the use of testing as one means of improving decision-making. Cronbach and Gleser (1957) have pointed out this fact anew for our present culture. They have specified that a chief purpose of testing should be the improvement of personnel decisions. Our culture depends on the placing of individuals in positions where they may most effectively contribute to specific needs. Thus, in education, achievement tests may help to place individuals in settings most congruent with their ability and provide the kind of stimulus needed for further growth. In business, testing may help to determine the individual who may most likely succeed in some kind of activity, whether it be administration, scientific research, etc.

But Ebel (1963) has noted that educational tests of aptitude and achievement are only one form of systematized observation and not a substitute for other kinds of evaluation. Ebel believes that testing may have some very real social consequences. He enumerates four, which are: 1) the fact that testing may place an indelible stamp of intellectual status on a child, thereby predetermining his social status as an adult and possibly doing considerable harm to his self-esteem and educational motivation; 2) that it may lead to an overly narrow conception of ability, thereby eliminating the diversity of talent sometimes associated with creativity; 3) that it may place the testers in a position to control education; and 4) that it may encourage impersonal, inflexible, and mechanistic processes of evaluation and determination, with a corresponding loss in essential human freedoms.

In recent years some attempt has been made to determine what is the objective influence of tests on the opportunities open to individuals, what part do test scores play in influencing the kinds of advice given to young people in schools, counseling agencies, and the like, and whether objective information about an individual's abilities has any special effect on the opinion the individual holds about himself. These questions have been asked by Goslin (1967) in an article dealing with the social consequences of testing. He reviews a number of surveys and research studies designed to provide some research information about the social consequences of testing. In one such study a number of counselors and teachers were asked to take a card sort test on which they had to make judgments about 28 fictitious students on the basis of test score data, grade averages, and the subjective evaluation of former teachers and advisers. This test (Hastings, 1960) was specifically designed to measure tendencies of the respondent to rely either on subjective factors, such as teacher comments, or objective criteria about the students, such as test scores, in deciding whether to place each pupil in a special advanced science test. Fourteen of the cases showed a congruence between objective and subjective data, and fourteen of the cases showed a discrepancy. Goslin indicated that the results of the study were inconclusive, leading to the implication that while counselors and teachers may possibly weigh objective test data properly, they interpret test results in relationship to other subjective data in a highly unpredictable manner. Thus, it would appear that understanding of test data and the role of test construction, etc., is not sufficient alone. Possibly, what may be needed is considerable more practice in weighing objective test scores in relationship to other behavioral data obtained by less rigorous means. It would appear that teachers' opinions are more inconsistent than those of counselors, but in both instances no clearly defined relationship could be predicted.

On the question of reporting test results to students and parents, neither counselors nor teachers showed a clear preference for either reporting scores or withholding them. Goslin points out that there is an obvious need for a more clearly defined policy in regard to the reporting of test results. However, a study by Rosenthal and Jacobson, summarized by Goslin, suggests that when first and second grade teachers are told to expect exceptional growth on the part of a randomly selected group of their students, exceptional leaps in I.Q. actually occur within the space of one year. Indirectly, this fact sheds some light on the question of teacher influence on intellectual growth. The whole thrust of modern social learning theory emphasizes the role which selective reinforcement can play in the development and maintenance of certain kinds of behavior. It may well be that knowledge of test scores and other information can bias a teacher either in favor of a child or against him. Certainly, knowledge of the academic or social status of the child's parents is a factor in the attitude which the teacher shows towards a child. If this is indeed the case, then the question of the self-fulfilling hypothesis becomes an important variable in individual differences. It would appear that test scores can help to increase the achievement potential and motivation of students who know that they are scoring highly and conversely can decrease the potential of individuals who learn that their scores are below average. In view of the complexities of test standardization and interpretation, it may well be that the lack of information is preferable to the biasing effect which comes from inadequate understanding of the meaning of test scores.

The influence of teachers and parents on the peer relations of the child is still another source of reinforcement. Research from social psychology provides corroboration of the fact that social reinforcement may be a most important factor in both achievement and the choice of specific vocational objectives. A vast amount of literature has been accumulated on the relationship of sociometric ratings to behavior (Gronlund, 1959). Sociometric choices have been related to measures of mental health, the California Test of Personality, the High School Personality Questionnaire, the Thematic Apperception Test, and the Rorschach (Bedoian, 1953; Guinouard and Ryschlak, 1959; Mussen and Porter, 1959; Tindall, 1955). They have been viewed as predictors of school dropout (Barclay, 1966b) and have been seen to be related to the sex and age of the teacher (Barclay, 1966c). These studies identify the importance that social acceptance has in relationship to actual achievement and aspiration level.

In addition, Backman and Secord (1962) and Backman, Secord and Pierce (1963) have indicated that peer group opinion is an important reinforcer in determining patterns of acceptable behavior and resistance to change. They have suggested that the greater the number of significant individuals (significant to the self) who are perceived to define an aspect of self congruently, the greater the resistance to change. These findings, related to the research regarding the educational environment and "press" which occurs in various environments, might suggest that the duration of stay in a given curriculum or the achievement production in that area is related to the perceived subjective congruence which exists between the individual and the supportive nurturance he obtains from his environment in the form of social reinforcement.

Summary

This chapter has been concerned with the relationship between testing and culture. The basic rationale of the chapter has related to the thesis that testing influences the course of culture and that culture itself can influence the nature of testing. Testing has been described as an objective and standardized attempt to make systematic evaluations of individuals and groups. The functions of testing have been traditionally related to the measurement of existing traits, qualities, aptitudes, intelligence, etc., as well as to the prediction of future patterns of behavior based on these measurements. The transition from evaluative measurement to prediction is a natural and easy one. However, the built-in limitations of testing, even in the descriptive phase of measurement, are vastly increased when prediction of future behavior is postulated.

Culture has been viewed as a series of mechanisms which are designed to ensure predictable patterns of consistent behavior from members of a group. With the disintegration of older mechanisms of cultural control and the acceleration of a technological culture based on mobility and industrial output, new mechanisms of control have emerged. Among these new mechanisms of control, both television and testing have assumed positions of considerable power potential. Both afford a kind of confidence or trust level which plays a systematic influence on the formation of attitudes and reinforces certain specific values in our society.

Stemming from the emergence of testing as a new means of cultural control, the social effects of testing are indicated. Children, teachers, parents, and business interests are influenced by the results of testing. This influence relates chiefly to the question of prediction of future behavior. However, the central problem of this prediction focuses on the fact that test predictors in the form of scores have often been implicitly, if not explicitly, considered immediate criteria of effective human behavior. Once this has occurred selective reinforcement procedures can accelerate differences in individuals, which can broadly be considered to be helpful to children scoring high on favorably considered test variables and to be somewhat harmful to those who score lower. Confronted with this kind of evidence it may well be that testing has a major influence on the differential motivation and aspiration level of various segments of our society.

3

....

Testing and the
Environmental Press

Testing in the previous chapter has been described in terms of an objective and scientific approach to making decisions about people. Moreover, the fact that there are numerous other methods of making such decisions has also been mentioned. Each method has its assets and liabilities. All methods are based on some type of observation, whether random or carefully determined. In addition, each method of making a decision about an individual or a group of individuals implicitly contains within it some reference to a criterion. In other words, there is some overt or covert measuring stick by which we make judgments about other people. In the unsystematic observation, certain behavioral data are interpreted to mean something. For example, when we walk down a corridor and a colleague fails to respond to our greeting, we can decide: 1) that he is angry at us about something or other, 2) that he is preoccupied and did not hear us, or 3) that an alternative judgment is appropriate in relation to what we already know about our interpersonal relationships. The same series of judgments is operating in a more systematic manner when an individual is interviewed for a position. In this instance, three or four staff members may interview an applicant either singly or in a group. They ask certain probing questions, note the applicant's appearance and interest in the situation, and explore areas of mutual interest or talk about people who may be known to each of them. This is an assessment procedure in which the responses of the applicant are being carefully weighed to determine whether he is the appropriate person to be hired. In this instance, each of the individuals interviewing the applicant will be looking for certain kinds of behavioral data which will be judged either as congruent or not congruent to certain criteria. Let us suppose that a new counselor is to be added to the staff of a school. After talking with the superintendent and the principal, the other members of the counseling staff are given an opportunity to meet the applicant. Perhaps one will be looking primarily at his background in testing. Another staff member will be interested in what his views are regarding personality counseling. Still another may view the new applicant as a threat to a position to which he is aspiring. The judgments of these staff members may then be different as they weigh the evidence accumulated in their interviews. Their final evaluation will be based not only on what they have seen and observed, but on their subjective evaluation of the criteria they are using as a means to their judgment.

The same process which is used with other kinds of decision making occurs as a confounding variable in the taking, use, and interpretation of tests. Although testing is a more objective means for obtaining a number of samples of behavior in a standardized manner, it still represents a problem in the assessment of individual differences within a social setting. Individuals approach testing with what has been referred to as a "set." Other individuals look at test results and make judgments with another "set." In the approach to testing, the taking of tests, and the interpretation of test results, a major variable which is generally outside the matter of test construction and validation is the environmental "press" which shapes and molds the expectations and values of those who either take or interpret tests.

It is the purpose of this chapter to consider a major variable in the assessment of human behavior through testing which has largely been overlooked or de-emphasized, despite the fact that it has been known for a long time. Reference is made to the construct of environmental press. By environmental press is meant the sum total of the environmental influences which shape, mold, and interact with the individual's perceptory notion of the world in which he lives. This is not to confound this notion with that of acquiescence, "yea saying," or the factors extracted from the Minnesota Multiphasic Inventory. The existence of a tendency for some individuals to acquiesce to a multiple choice personality inventory is indeed an example of the end product of en-

vironmental press but is not itself to be confounded with it.[4] Environmental press is a term used to denote the *process* whereby acquiescence
may be considered a real factor in the taking of certain types of tests.
It is very likely the uncontrolled source of variance which accounts for
a large percentage of the individual differences that are obtained on
standardized intelligence, achievement and personality tests. It is the
major scaffolding behind differences in personality inventories identified as results of social acquiescence or response set. It is the relatively
unexplored frontier which will add an important dimension of meaning to the interpretation of testing results of many standardized and
objective test instruments.

Theoretical Rationale

There is mounting evidence today that social desirability, *i.e.*, the
stimulus value that an individual has for those around him, is related
to the responses that he makes in social learning situations. Earlier
historical approaches described the relationship of social stimulus to
social response through the mediation of internal mental states or
dimensions. Brentano's *Intentionale Inexistenz* (1873) and Freud's
concept of cathexis (1953) are examples of this approach.[5] Other more
recent approaches have been Lewin's field theory (1936), Roger's self-
concept theory (1951, 1961), Heider's theory of interpersonal behavior

---

[4] Block (1965), in the *Challenge of Response Sets*, has discussed the literature
and meaning of two responses styles, acquiescence and desirability, which appear
to be important dimensions in the interpretation of multiple-choice personality
inventories. Essentially, this suggests that the tendency to agree with items or to
respond in a manner which will convey the most favorable impression are variables
which should be considered in test interpretation.

[5] Brentano began this chain of thought with his doctrine of intentionality, in
which he postulated that each individual sees the world of reality through the
mediation of his own perception. This act of perception he called the intentional
image. The intentional image involves not only a primary object relationship to
outer reality but also a secondary object relationship to the mind. This position,
it has been argued (Barclay, 1959, 1964), was developed and adapted by Brentano's student, Sigmund Freud, in his doctrine of cathexis. A cathexis in Freudian
terminology referred to the idea of physical energy being lodged or attached to
mental structures or processes somewhat on the analogy of the electric charge. The
phenomenological contributions of the Wurzburg school and the experimental
studies of Wertheimer with the phi phenomenon led to the development of Gestalt
psychology. Koehler offered the postulate of isomorphism to explain the relationship of perception to the outer world of reality. He suggested that all experienced
order in space and time is replicated by a corresponding order within the cortex.
Lewin's position was that each individual exerted a valence which both affected
and was perceived by others in his field. More recently, Heider, in the phenomenological tradition of Brentano and Husserl, has examined the relationship of
language concepts and meanings as they are held and understood by individuals
with certain contextual settings. Finally, Kelly has held that for effective interaction, persons must accurately construe the outlook of each other.

(1958), Wylie's thorough review and resolution of phenomenological positions toward the self-concept (1961), the ideas of Kelly (1963) about role and its constructs, Osgood's (1957) work with the semantic differential, and Festinger's theory of cognitive dissonance (1957). They all point to the importance of social interaction in the determination of the unique personal goals that the individual sets for himself and the way in which he perceives himself.

These positions, despite a wide variation of theoretical orientations, all accent the importance of subjective modes of perception in the formation of behavioral repertories and responses. They emphasize the central important role of perception as the unique subjective means whereby reality is interpreted and assessed and survival assured. However, all of them, and this is the important point, state that the subjective productions within the mind are the result of social interactions. This specific point — that even though perception may be the key to individual behavior, the manner in which perception is formed is a question of social learning — has been the contribution of more recent theorists and experimental investigators. Piaget (1952) has enunciated the twofold principle of assimilation and accommodation which he believes governs the perceptual development of the child. Some experiences are assimilated into the structure of the self. Others, to which the individual accommodates himself, are those which he cannot assimilate. Thus, whatever may be the neurological implications of how perception affects the cortex, it would appear that characteristic modes of responding to social stimuli begin early to create what Skinner would term operant conditioning. Nor is it simply the response system of the individual operating on a pleasure-pain continuum that shapes perceptual behavior. There is a constant feedback from the reactions and responses of others. Though the neurological aspects of perception are chiefly derived deductively today, there is evidence that the brain-stem reticular activating system which spreads its fibres throughout the brain-stem and into the thalamus plays a vital part in both learning and perception. According to Berlyne (1960), it includes ascending pathways to all areas of the cortex and descending pathways to motor areas. It appears more concerned with the urgency of stimuli than with their specific properties and may excite the whole cortex. Taylor (1962), citing the work of Pavlov, thinks that the brain-stem reticular activating system at first relays impulses from any sense receptor to any part of the cortex and that later cortical differentiations appear through a process of conditioned responses. Pavlov felt that the main function of the cortex was the establishment of temporary connections that he recognized to be specific to the individual organism, probably initiated by random behavior and conditioned by rewarding responses.

Whether this theoretical analysis is correct or not, it would appear, given the fact of neurological integration, that most early perception and perceptory learning is mediated by visual stimulation more than by any other sense modality. The child's early responses are gradually tied down by the social and personal reinforcers of things such as the mother's smile or the sense of well-being which results from sensory gratification.

The studies of Bandura and Walters (1963) have emphasized the role that social imitation, modeling, and shaping of behavior by adults and peers have on the formation of a behavior repertory. Backman and Secord (1962) and Backman, Secord and Pierce (1963) have indicated that peer group opinions are important social reinforcers in determining patterns of acceptable behavior and resistance to change. The question of whether a given individual will change his behavior is directly related to whether his friends appraise him through disapproval of specific behavioral acts. Kaufman (1962), in an experimental study based in part on Festinger's theory of cognitive dissonance, suggested that conflicting perceptions in the individual in response to certain behavioral stimuli can result in a situation of ambivalence and often avoidance. The organism attempts to bring about some kind of psychic or mental homeostasis either by compromise behaviors or avoidance reactions. Kaufman found that if a subject values an attribute highly but conceives of himself as possessing very little of it, a state of imbalance will exist and will persist until he enhances the degree to which he sees himself as possessing the attribute or lowers the value he attributes to it. These studies, taken together, would support the notion that the analysis of childhood behavior requires a recognition and understanding not only of the paramount importance of subjective perception, but also of the fact that these perceptions are formed early in reaction to social reinforcers and sustained through the medium of social learning. Relating this to testing and test interpretation, it is easy to conclude that testing as an experience in itself and test information feed-back can be significant factors in molding the behavior repertory of both teachers, parents, students, and others who may view these test results.

Specifically, then, there is evidence that the process of individual response development in social learning situations is mediated by the environmental "press."

The Nature of Environmental "Press"

The concept of environmental "press" refers to the sum total of environmental or cultural factors which come to bear upon the shaping and molding of individual behavior in a given setting. It includes not only a process whereby certain behavioral responses are learned and assimilated, but also a process of discrimination based on learned responses and anticipated responses within a given environmental setting. Children learn how to behave in relationship to aggression. Sometimes fathers suggest they fight; other times they are taught to arbitrate their differences. As they grow older, they learn to filter out the various stimuli in a given situation and accommodate to them by what they judge to be an appropriate response. The careful modeling of human behavior is learned early. Learning of emotional responses often precedes the emergence of cognitive styles of expression. Our earliest mental reactions are not verbalized, but we feel a wide range of love and hate before we can think. And this emotional aspect of our personality is formed very early and continues to develop throughout our life. Our earliest formation or the earliest shaping of our behaviors comes from the affection or lack of affection which our parents, and particularly mothers, have for their children. The tender episodes of nursing, cradling, fondling, and singing to the child convey a sense of security and well being to him and aid in the development of an appropriate response repertory. On the contrary, a child also responds to anxiety, implicit or explicit rejection, hostility, and inconsistency of treatment. As he grows, he develops as a complex computer which is being continually programmed by the environment.

Culture transmits patterns of behavior in a very systematic manner. Even as hereditary characteristics are transmitted through minute biological combinations which specify the direction, sequencing, and evolution of development, so culture as a mechanism of group defense and survival relies on the direct agency of certain segments of the population. The family, the peer group, laws, customs, religious precepts all play an important role in the transmission of the cultural patterns. These cultural agencies utilize principles of learning in a relatively unsystematic manner to transmit behavior. They shape behavior by praise and punishment, provide exemplary models to emulate or imitate, and continually mold the development of the individual. Thus a child learns to hate those people his parents hate and to like those who are liked by them. He becomes afraid of people who are different, whose skin is a different color, or who show differential characteristics. The child absorbs almost unconsciously the inclinations and aversions of the adults with whom he is in frequent contact. Usually, his affective life is directly reflected by the attitudes and models provided for him. As a child, he attempts to respond to the shaping behavior of others by conforming to their expectations, and in his later life he may never feel the need to reevaluate his attitudes.

These attitudes, emotions, and feeling tones are derived from the shaping effect which is continually going on around us. We are, in a very real sense, what our parents and society make us. To paraphrase the statement of a popular anonymous poem, if a child lives with criticism, he learns how to condemn others. If he lives with tolerance, he learns how to be tolerant; if he lives with fairness, he learns what justice is; and if people like him, he learns to like others.

We learn behavior through the continued shaping effect of the environment. The environment reinforces those responses which others consider appropriate for their expectations of our behavior. We learn that if we are to obtain approval of ourselves, we must learn to make certain kinds of responses to certain kinds of social expectations and stimuli. Through a process of operant conditioning, we learn the successful and unsuccessful approximation responses to the anticipations of others. The reactions of peers and teachers are soon joined to this basic reinforcement system. Ultimately, the laws and customs of society are also internalized to some degree. From this kind of reinforcement, we learn to generalize certain response repertories so that we can apply them to new situations. We also learn how to make discriminatory judgments in which we decide whether a particular possible response to a situation is better than an alternative response. Ultimately, we accommodate our behaviors to the cultural environment in which we live.

These facts about the nature of the environmental "press" have been known for some time. However, it is only in recent years that an attempt has been made to measure the effects of the environmental press. The approach first was developed by researchers in the psychology of vocational development in an effort to more precisely delineate effective criteria of behavior in a collegiate setting. Super (1951) suggested the broad guidelines for some of this research. He stated that the appropriateness of an individual's choice in a given occupation or vocational curriculum depends on the particular configuration of his abilities, personality characteristics, and interests as measured against the specific demands of a given vocation. Tiedeman, Bryan and Rulon (1953) and Tiedeman (1954) devised a method of reflecting choice patterns by the use of a centour score. This is explained by Cole, Wilson and Tiedeman (1964) as

> a percentile-type statement which is a function of the probability that the alternative chosen by an individual with a particular pattern of traits will be of a specific kind. The higher the centour score, the higher the relative frequency of a pattern of scores among those for a group of individuals who have made a specific choice.

From these beginnings, others began to accumulate evidence that the process of individual response development in social learning situations is also mediated by the environmental "press." The research of Pace and Stern (1958), Thistlethwaite (1958, 1960), Nichols and Holland (1963), and Astin (1964b, 1964c) with the environmental assessment technique lends credence to the notion that the specific pattern of social responses in individuals is shaped by the social behavior of those dominating the environment. The process of shaping is referred to as "press." That such "presses" exist in the school setting is unquestionable. The expectations of teachers, their differential biases (derived in turn often from their academic background), their patterns of reinforcing student responses, the reactions of peers and their mutual reinforcement procedures, and the influence of parents and administration all directly or indirectly shape the behavioral responses of individuals who remain in that environment by choice or necessity.

Measurement of the Environmental Press

The measurement of the environmental press has been approached differently by groups of individuals. Pace and Stern (1958), Thistlethwaite (1958, 1960), Nichols and Holland (1963), and Astin (1964b, 1964c, 1965) have attempted to find more adequate criteria regarding the nature of effective human behavior in a given environment. Lee (1951), Kirk (1958), Bloom (1964), Wolf (1964), and Fifer (1964) have tended to look at social class and cultural group differences as they indirectly reflect environmental forces. The general approach of both of these groups of theorists reflects a common concern that many of the differences obtained on testing instruments do not reflect inherent differences in individuals as much as they are largely the results of specific environmental conditions. Thus, the search for measurement of the environment is related to the development of a more adequate system of criteria. What constitutes effective human behavior? Can this be identified without constant reference to the cultural milieu? All of the above researchers would seem to agree that it cannot. In short, testing does not provide its own criteria of performance.

The first group of researchers have developed their findings in relation to the question of finding a more adequate set of criteria for higher education. Past research in higher education has tended to settle on three combinations of predictors and three combinations of criteria. Test instrument scores, grade-point average, or other scores were used as predictors of success in college. These typically were obtained from high school achievement. For both predictors and criteria there have been intellective ones, nonintellective ones, and combinations of both. Intellective predictors are those which tap essentially verbal and abstract abilities and generally indicate how well certain specific types of information and problem-solving techniques have been mastered. In intellective predictors, a good deal of emphasis is placed on the student's ability to recall facts and procedures which can be measured and scored objectively. The common intellective predictors that have been used in forecasting student collegiate success are aptitude and intelligence test scores, achievement scores, rank in high school graduating class, and high school grade average either in one subject or globally considered. Nonintellective predictors take into consideration various theorized dimensions of personality, motivation, and interest patterns. A variety of such tests have been used, including personality and motivational tests, interest inventories, interviews and personal ratings, biographical information, study habit inventories, self-appraisals and peer nomination techniques, adjective checklists, semantic differentials, and measures of self-concept.

Many of the current testing batteries, particularly the personality inventories, were *not* specifically designed to measure effective human behavior in the collegiate setting. That they measure something is undoubtedly true, but the point is that in many instances, the connection between the scores obtained on these instruments and effective collegiate behavior is unclear. There are seldom clear descriptions of the empirically observed behavior which is related positively or negatively to testing dimensions. However, in all fairness to many investigators, the problems in designing adequate tests and obtaining adequate test predictors are primarily related to the question of determining adequate criteria. The fact that colleges and universities place their overwhelming confidence in a specific form of intellectual criterion, the academic grade-point average, is both understandable and damning to the effort of researchers to increase predictive and longitudinal validity for their test instruments. For a grade-point average does not begin to reflect adequately the comprehensive cluster of positively correlated or negatively correlated behaviors which are related to success or failure in given settings.

This reliance on intellective criteria is understandable because college faculties are very prone to accept the intellectual achievement indicated by the grade-point average as *the* criterion of college success *par excellence.* Faculty members all know, or think they know, what a grade means. Added to this is the difficulty of obtaining any reasonable consensus from faculty members on what constitutes a nonintellective criterion of college or university success. Some suggestions that have been made for nonintellective criteria of collegiate success are participation in extracurricular affairs, feelings of satisfaction with college experience as rated by the student or others, peer group judgments, leadership ratings, creativity ratings, aspiration statements, clarification of vocational goals, dropout status versus that of staying in, religious, political and social attitudes and values, and post-college criteria, such as listings in "Who's Who," admission to or success in graduate school, membership in professional societies, publications, and community status. When this list of nonintellective criteria is reviewed, it is understandable why the institutions of higher learning have tended to place high confidence in the grade-point average earned by the student. It is easily obtained, pin-points success in terms of a concrete criterion, and provides an immediate recognition of those values in which college and university communities tend to place most confidence. Fishman and Parsanella (1960), in reviewing 580 studies relating to various combinations of intellective and nonintellective predictors and criteria of collegiate success, point out that 408 or 70 percent of all these studies concentrated only on intellective predictors and intellective criteria.

The Environmental Press in the Collegiate Setting

The studies of Holland (1958, 1959a, 1959b, 1960, 1961, 1962, 1963, 1964, 1966), Holland and Nichols (1963, 1964), Astin (1963, 1964b, 1964c, 1965), Astin and Holland (1961, 1962), Astin and Nichols (1964), and Thistlethwaite (1958, 1960) are characterized by a search for a new set of predictor and criterion variables within the collegiate setting. They have postulated that the learning environment itself is a measurable criterion which is independent of testing protocols and other criteria.

Their studies have been characterized by extensive statistical analyses of large samples available to Holland and Astin first through the National Merit Scholarship Corporation and more recently in the American College Testing Program. The theoretical posture upon which the studies are based is explained by Holland (1962) as follows:

> The theory assumes that at the time a person chooses a vocation, he is the product of his heredity and a variety of environmental forces including peers, parents and other significant adults, social class, American culture, and the physical environment. Out of his experiences, he develops a hierarchy of orientations for coping with environmental tasks; this hierarchy may be referred to as the pattern of personal orientations. Each of these orientations is related to a particular physical or social environment and to a particular set of abilities. The person making a vocational choice in a sense 'searches' for those environments which are congruent with his personal orientation.

Holland postulates that people who are successful in different occupations tend to differ in basic personality attributes. He has isolated six categories of personality attributes or types: Realistic, Intellectual, Social, Conventional, Enterprising, and Artistic. For each type he has developed a model orientation, a theoretical complex of personal traits, coping mechanisms, vocational and educational goals, aptitudes, and previous history. The extent to which a person resembles any model orientation is called his personal orientation for that type; his total pattern with respect to all six model orientations is his pattern of personal orientations.

These six categories are then used not only to describe the personal orientations of individuals but also to assess the pattern of orientations of various occupational classes. Holland (1964) hypothesizes that career choice then consists of moving toward the occupational group whose members have personal orientations like one's own:

> In short, occupational language and behavior have been construed in terms of personality; these procedures make it possible to talk about vocational choice, vocational behavior, and achievement in terms of personal variables. Thus, occupational classes designate types of people and, similarly, vocational choice becomes a function of personality. By regarding a person's interests, occupation, and vocational knowledge as information about his personality, we can integrate a broad range of human behavior in a single theory of personality and thus avoid the need for separate theories of 'interest' and 'personality.'

Within any particular class of occupations, Holland (1959a) feels that the level of choice made by an individual is a function of both his intelligence and his self-evaluation. Thus, knowing a person's pattern of personal orientations, his approximate intellectual level, and his self-evaluation (to be obtained from scales of occupational content), some predictions about appropriate career choices can be made.

To enable him to test his vocational choice theory, Holland (1959b) developed an occupational index, the Vocational Preference Inventory (VPI), which is essentially a list of occupational titles. An individual indicates which occupations he likes and dislikes, and from his pattern of answers the pattern of personal orientations is derived. Using this scale, as well as high school and college grades, examples of creativity (such as original musical, artistic, or scientific work), participation in school activities, and family data, Holland and his associates have done a series of longitudinal studies on National Merit Scholarship finalists since 1958. Predictive studies have thus been obtained, as well as comparisons between dropouts and those who remain and between intelligent and creative students.

An early study (Holland 1959a) dealt with the prediction of college grades from scores on the California Personality Inventory and the Scholastic Aptitude Test. It was found that the verbal and mathematics scores on the SAT serve equally well as predictors of college freshman grades. On the CPI, the most predictive validity is obtained from the Sp (social presence) and So (sociability) scales. As one might expect, the combination yielded better predictors than any one test separately. The study also seems to show that both personality and intellectual factors are involved in academic success.

Next Holland (1960) tried to predict college grades among National Merit Scholars through the use of the 16 Personality Factor Test, his own Vocational Preference Inventory, the National Merit Student Survey (an experimental personality inventory filled out by applicants), the Scholastic Aptitude Test, and high school grades. The best individual predictor turned out to be high school grades. But nonintellectual factors from the various scales, including the 16 Personality Factor scales relating to superego, persistence, and deferred gratification, were useful in predicting academic achievement. A major conclusion of these studies was that nonintellectual factors emerge as more predictive of academic success when ability and aptitude factors are controlled by a selection process.

Holland then studied the personality variables present in creative and in academically able students. The sample was again composed of National Merit finalists. Comparisons were made among high school records, answers in a 16-item questionnaire dealing with creative endeavors on the high school level, and 72 parental, personal, and demographic variables obtained from applications for the competition and from the participating high schools. The statistical analysis of the variables revealed the following pattern: creative adolescents can be characterized as independent, intellectual, expressive, asocial, consciously original, and having high achievement aspirations. By contrast, non-creative high achievers are persevering, sociable, responsible, and have parents with more authoritarian values and attitudes. In this particular study (1961) Holland also found a negligible relationship between academic achievement and creativity (it must, of course, be remembered that this was already a high-achievement sample) and that teachers in general rated academic achievers more highly than creative students.

The next step consisted of finding out what family variables might have contributed to the personality development and career choice of high aptitude students (Holland and Nichols, 1963). A random sample of National Merit finalists and their parents from the 1960 competition was polled by mail. Parents were asked about child-rearing attitudes and aspirations for their children; students were asked about positions of leadership they had held and their accomplishments in science, music, art, drama, and writing. In general, a negative relationship was found between parents' preferences for realistic, conventional, and social occupations and their children's achievement in some phase of the arts. On the other hand, easygoing child-rearing attitudes correlated positively with children's artistic achievement. The investigators concluded that in general a child will not achieve highly in an area in which his parents show little or no interest. One interesting sidelight was that for both sexes the variables contributed by the father were more closely related to the child's achievement than were those coming from the mother. This runs counter to the assumptions generally made in child-rearing studies and, if true, may have some interesting implications.

Astin and Nichols (1964) studied over 5,000 college seniors of high ability to see whether there were differences not only of personality but of life goals between those preparing for various occupations. A factor-analysis yielded seven factors of importance: self-esteem, scholarship, personal comforts, prestige, altruism, artistic motivation, and science-technology. Dividing the total group into 36 occupational subgroups, Astin and Nichols found great differences between the groups in the relative strength of the seven factors.

As a result of this study, Astin and Holland then have continued to investigate the comparative environment of various colleges on the assumption that if occupational groups vary in personal traits, then college environments will also vary according to the proportion of majors in various occupational fields in attendance at each. The Environmental Assessment Technique (EAT), a method of assessing the college environment on the basis of eight characteristics of the student body, was developed. The eight characteristics include size of student body, intelligence level of the students, and the personal orientations of the students as measured by Holland's six categories: Realistic, Intellectual, Social, Conventional, Enterprising, and Artistic.

The EAT has been validated both against Pace and Stern's College Characteristics Index (Astin and Holland, 1961) and against data received from seniors at the various institutions giving in questionnaire form a retrospective view of the college environment (Astin, 1963). On the basis of both these studies, its authors feel assured of construct validity. Reliability studies using the EAT were done for a six year period with all of these colleges and resulted in reliability coefficients generally in the .90 range.

Astin therefore used the EAT, again in conjunction with personal and family data, Scholastic Aptitude scores, and results of the California Test of Personality, to compare dropouts with those remaining in school during the fourth year of college (Astin, 1964b). The purposes of the study were to determine if particular characteristics of a college environment had any effect on the dropout rate and to see what personality variables were involved for each of the two groups. He found that none of the college characteristics had any greater influence upon the rate of male dropouts but that females had a greater tendency to drop out in a school that had a relatively high proportion of male students. As for personality measures, the study shows dropouts to be more aloof, self-centered, assertive, and interested in personal pleasure than "stay-ins." Astin points out that in admitting students to institutions of higher education, personality variables and not just scholastic proficiency should be used as predictors. Furthermore, dropouts should be studied more intensively, and they should be classified according to the reasons for leaving school.

Two recent studies done with the Environmental Assessment Technique have been concerned with determining the characteristics of entering student bodies in colleges (Astin, 1964c) and determining the characteristics of the colleges to which they go (Astin, 1965). In the first of these, a short questionnaire was given to all entering freshmen in 248 colleges in the fall of 1961. Scores from these, plus some information obtained from the institutions about their students, were factor-analyzed to yield six major characteristics of entering freshman classes. These were: Intellectualism, Estheticism, Status, Leadership, Pragmatism, and Masculinity. Astin thinks that these represent a meaningful way of describing the characteristics of entering freshmen and can be useful in the process of advising students about college choice.

To carry this process one step further, he then repeated the study with entering freshmen at 1015 colleges and universities to get scores for each institution on the six freshman input factors, and he computed the six personal orientations plus size and intelligence (the eight EAT factors) for each institution (Astin, 1965). These results are available as T scores in a table listing all of these institutions, approximately 5/6 of all the colleges in the United States. Thus, for the first time counselors and advisors will be able to help prospective college students with information not only about the course offerings, costs, or degree programs, but also to offer them some information about the personality and environmental factors that make colleges unique. Whether the practical application of the technique will live up to its promise remains to be seen. Nevertheless, the methods of measuring both student and institutional personality variables developed by Holland and Astin represent a new and creative step forward in the study and practical application of personality and career choice variables.

Measurement of the High School Environment

Holland and Astin have not generalized beyond their data. They indicate the differences which they have found but at this point have not yet extended their analysis of environments to high schools. They point out the fact that freshmen entering college already have a definable profile of vocational interests which are related to personality characteristics. They also indicate that colleges and universities extend their influence through similar presses. How these presses are maintained can be subsumed under a consideration of social-behavioral learning theory. Holland has pointed out that individuals with a certain preference for intellectualism tend to find their way into curricula which express this press. They may, for example, be attracted to the biological sciences. They have certain expectations about what professors may require of them. Conversely, professors in that field represent a generally homogenous approach to their field (despite individual differences). Although learning is chiefly evaluated through the mechanism of testing, other criteria of evaluation relating to the congruence of a student's behavior to the model conceptualized by the professor play a heavy role in predisposing professors to mark liberally or harshly, to endorse wholeheartedly or damn with faint praise. Explicitly or implicitly, the student, if he is to survive — and this is particularly true in graduate studies — must learn to acquiesce to the model proposed to him by his major professors. Unfortunately, the nature and direction of these models and presses are generally unknown to the secondary student. By a process of trial and error he must learn *after* he enters a collegiate institution which of these cultural transmissions is most congruent to his own needs and aspirations. By the same token, the student in vocational education is seldom aware of the specific environmental press criteria by which he will be judged when he enters the world of work. This ambiguity about the real nature of the challenges which are ahead for the secondary student may be one of the prime reasons for the indifferent motivation which many high school students manifest. Concrete information about their own characteristics, as related to specific fields of interest which may be congruent with these characteristics, would not only help the students to be more realistic in the choice of an occupation but would help vocational counselors to make some real power predictions about expected success or failure.

If the foregoing rationale is correct, then the differential presses found in collegiate curricula should find their counterparts in the secondary curriculum. What is more logical than to suspect that the foreign language teacher, who by virtue of her assignment upholds one sector of the intellectual spectrum, should reflect the kinds of presses to which she herself was subject and which she has found through teaching to become a strong operant in maintaining this behavior? This should be true for many different areas in the high school curriculum.

In a study of the secondary "press" (Barclay, 1967a) the writer attempted to determine what were the characteristics of the environmental press in a high school setting. Building upon the rationale of Holland that certain environmental presses are felt and incorporated into the behavior repertories of individuals who succeed in a given environment, it was reasoned that such attitudes and values should be implicit in the criteria of excellence which different teachers set for their students. In other words, because of the existence of differences within the environmental press in the college setting, it would be reasonable to expect such differences to be perpetuated within the high school curriculum. Thus the rationale for the existence of measurable dimensions in the environment was considered to operate as a set of circumstances which would be revealed in traditional personality testing instruments. Building upon the expected biases, it was hypothesized that these differences would be measurable on personality type instruments. The criterion used in this study was the teachers' own judgment of what constitutes an effective student in their curriculum.

In conjunction with the Oakland, California, Public Schools' vocational curriculum follow-up study of 1965, each senior teacher in each of the following curricula was asked to nominate the three individuals in his or her class who best or least met his own standards of performance. The curriculum areas were: 1) Art, 2) Business Education, 3) English, 4) Foreign Languages, 5) Home Making, 6) Industrial Arts, 7) Mathematics, 8) Music, 9) Physical Education, 10) Science, and 11) Social Science. They were also asked to nominate the three students who least met these qualifications. In all, 2165 nominations were obtained on senior students. These students had been tested on some eighty personality, intellectual, and vocational variables.[6] The test data available for high and low rated students were then analyzed.

---

[6] These variables included Holland's Vocational Inventory, Farquhar's Motivation Scales, the California Psychological Inventory, a Socio-Economic Index, and the Minnesota Vocational Interest Inventory, together with SCAT and STEP Scores and Grade Point Averages in each field and by year.

The findings of this study revealed many significant differences both within the high and low ratings in each curriculum and between highly rated individuals in different curricula. The findings obtained in this manner were then compared with the results obtained by Holland in two studies reported in 1966 (Holland, 1966). In these studies, Holland undertook to verify a classification scheme based on his vocational inventory. This classification system was based on scale scores derived from a list of occupational preferences and titles. To take the inventory, a student indicates which occupations he likes and dislikes. Scores on only the following 14 item scales were used: Realistic, Intellectual, Social, Conventional, Enterprising, and Artistic. The scales and their general interpretation are as follows:

Scale	Code No.	Preference for:
Realistic	1	technical and skilled trades
Intellectual	2	scientific occupations
Social	3	teaching and helping occupations
Conventional	4	clerical occupations
Enterprising	5	supervisory and sales occupations
Artistic	6	artistic, musical, and literary occupations

In Holland's studies, a classification system was analyzed in terms of preference expressed both by college-bound youth in vocations in the Spring of 1964 and a follow-up in the Fall of 1964. The classification system simply provides for the coding of the above scales in a manner similar to that used by the Minnesota Multiphasic Personality Inventory, *i.e.*, the highest score is cited first, the next highest second, and the third highest third. This code system then was found to differentiate between vocational preferences (in the first survey) and to be basically substantiated by individuals who entered certain academic fields in the following Fall (second survey). Holland is cautious in generalizing his research findings to the high school curriculum, though the samples included some 12,000 college-bound youth in the first study and over 10,000 students in nine representative colleges and universities in the second study.

The writer, using the same coding system, found similar profiles existing in the curricula of the high school. The greatest similarities were, of course, in curricula which expressed the college bound youth rather than the vocational or terminal high school student. Highly rated students in foreign languages, science, and mathematics tend to have similar profiles receiving a high scaled score on intellectualism. They also show a high mean score on the California Psychological Inventory scales of achievement via conformity, responsibility, and socialization. Their motivation level as measured by Farquhar's scales is at a very high level. Even students rated as least conforming to the concept of effective students by foreign language teachers far exceed the mean motivation scores of highly rated students in other curricula. Space does not allow for a full discussion of the differences or profiles obtained in this study. Suffice it to say here that evidence is presented which validates the existence of differential environmental presses toward learning in the various high school curricula. Teachers in various curricula reflect more or less accurately the environmental press which they themselves acquired in their collegiate or university training. Their choices of students who reflect what they consider to be effective human behavior in their curriculum indicate indirectly what is the nature of the learning press they sustain and reinforce in their classes.

The existence of differential secondary presses appears to be confirmed by this study. The present status of knowledge about the nature of social behavioral learning in relationship to cultural transmission suggests that the cultural transmission is reflected by agents who, through an infinite variety of modeling, reinforcement continencies, value judgments, and a continued flow of exemplary models in both the curriculum and interpersonal relations, bring pressure to bear upon children. This means simply that certain characteristics, personal, motivational, and vocational, are coupled with academic achievement in reaching some kind of consensus or congruence with the subjective criteria of excellence in effective human behavior.

An Approach to the Measurement of Elementary School Environment

To what extent, it may be asked, is it possible to extend the measurement of the environmental press to the elementary school level? For surely, if high school students are aware of differential presses which mold them and their behavior, there must be evidence of the existence of such a press in the elementary school setting. In keeping with the basic rationale that a culture transmits its behavioral goals through agents, one would expect to find the teacher and peers exerting a directional press through social learning. For teachers and peers constitute immediate criteria of effective behavior in the elementary classroom.

In a series of studies over a number of years, the writer has investigated the measurement of the environmental press in the elementary school classroom. In order to measure this press, it is necessary to obtain test information regarding the peer ratings of students toward each other and the concurrent evaluation of the teacher toward each child. To this end the writer has utilized sociometry and teachers' ratings, as well as a variety of other experimental instruments such as a semantic differential, interest inventories, measures of perceptual distortion and integration, and, more recently, a modified version of Holland's Vocational Inventory with a self-competency scale.

Despite the evidence which supports the close relationship of sociometric phenomena to a wide range of personality dimensions (see Gronlund, 1959, for voluminous details on the research), sociometry is still not used widely in the schools. Why is this so? Certainly the earlier studies in sociometry have provided much information about the parameters of the sociometric phenomenon. But as is true in much of the earlier counseling and school psychology research, often the wrong questions have been explored. Much of the previous research in sociometry is characterized as: 1) too localized in nature with preoccupation over the plotting of elaborate charts and concentric circles, whose function possesses little logical power potential for classroom teachers; 2) too prone to explore irrelevant criteria of choice-making (e.g., friends for a birthday party); 3) too inadequate in terms of working out economical and easily comprehended means of comparing groups (e.g., complex matrices which are not understood by school personnel, analysis of mutual choices, etc.); and 4) too short-sighted through its failure to utilize sociometric elections in terms of longitudinal prediction, the introduction of differential treatment procedures, and the recognition that sociometric elections can be used as a criterion of behavior change.

In a series of studies with sociometric devices, the writer found that sociometric scores were related to measured indices of perceptual development or distortion (Barclay and Barclay, 1965), were longitudinal predictors of school dropouts (Barclay, 1966b), were subject to variations depending on the sex and age of the teachers (Barclay, 1966c), were related to a variety of interest patterns in and out of school (Barclay, 1966a), and could be used as measures of behavioral change in relationship to the introduction of remedial treatment procedures in the classroom (Barclay, 1967).[7]

Some of the information contained in these studies is not startlingly new, but the notion of measuring the environmental press through sociometry is new. The rationale of this approach has been detailed by the writer in an article entitled "Sociometry: Rationale and Technique for Effecting Behavior Change in the Elementary School" (1966). As Bandura (1963) has pointed out, attitudes toward learning are largely the result of a specific pattern of social reinforcements for certain kinds of responses. Children learn social reponses toward learning by the imitation of social models and by a process of continuing

---

[7] These studies involve over 3500 elementary and junior high school students in Michigan, Idaho, and California.

personal psychological approximation wherein they acquiesce to the approved responses which are upheld by their teachers and fellow students.

In a study by Jackson and Forsyth (1966), Holland's Vocational Preference Inventory was adapted to the elementary school population and tried out on four classes of fifth graders. The results of this study indicated that the inventory could be used with some modifications at the elementary school level as well as in college and secondary levels. Though the results must be considered tentative at this time, experimentation is presently being conducted utilizing third, fourth, fifth, and sixth graders to determine the nature of derived dimensions of Holland's Inventory in relationship to sociometric phenomena and teachers' ratings. It is hypothesized that classroom congruence in learning goals will be related to the predominance of one or other environmental press in the classroom. To the extent that there are conflicting environmental presses, the social and academic goals of learning may be endangered.

Summary

The meaning of the notion of the environmental press and the research studies which have been cited in this chapter should be clear to the counselor. Essentially what is being said is that environmental press is a complex series of forces which shape and mold the perceptual apparatus of individuals. Perception is both an active shaping force on the response repertory of individuals and the product of reinforced behavior. The response repertory of an individual is clearly the product of a long series of learned behavior derived from social settings. Moreover, though researchers distinguish between various kinds of learning, in practice one cannot separate what is cognitively learned in terms of knowledge and skills from the social context in which that learning takes place. It is then understandable how college students who find themselves in a curriculum essentially not congruent with their attitudes and behaviors will seek another curriculum more appropriate. It is likewise understandable how high school and elementary school children may tend not only to reject peers who represent an environmental press to which they are unwilling to submit, but also to reject those academic goals and criteria of excellence associated with their rejected peers. The child who finds his social stimulus and response repertory to be consistently not congruent with others or with the implied criteria of the learning situation will find it most difficult to intellectually or socially assimilate these criteria and direct his behavior towards that end. This may well be one of the prime causes for the large group of educationally alienated children who refuse to demonstrate the motivation necessary to achieve in verbal learning.

If the research on environmental press be accepted, then there is a necessity to re-evaluate all testing results in achievement, intelligence, personality, and interest areas. For test scores reflect cultural differences and will have to be evaluated within a cultural framework. Without such a proper coding of the dimensions of testing, the comparability of test scores for one group with those of another lies open to serious questioning.

4

The Criterion Problem in Using
and Interpreting Tests

Initially in this monograph a number of specific issues in testing were posed which had been the focus of both popular and serious criticisms in recent years. Specific responses were provided to some of these specific issues. But the overriding problem in both the construction of tests and the application of test results to various dimensions of human behavior has been the criterion problem. This can be most clearly illustrated by an analysis of the uses of testing. Tests have been used in counseling for evaluation, assessment, prediction, and research purposes. Within counseling, there is a tendency towards a shift from the use of tests to supplement clinical judgment of the characteristics of an individual to the use of tests and test information as a basis for counselor-client decision-making. This is an excellent development and allows for both counselor and client to determine the level of criteria to be used in the decision-making process. Tests have also been used more often as criterion measures for the selection of candidates for an institution of higher learning and for the placement of individuals in certain sections of curricula within public schools. This aspect of the use of tests relates to the concept of prediction. Basically, there is an assumption (very largely warranted) that the best guarantee of future behavior is based on past and present behavioral modes. Finally, tests of all kinds have been used as criterion measures in research studies. It is argued that if a test is valid and reliable, it can be used as a measure of dependent variable changes ascribed to a specific treatment procedure. For example, if an adjustment test is considered to be a valid and reliable measure of personal adjustment, a standard research procedure would be to administer the test to a group of children, randomly assign sub-groups to different treatment procedures, such as group counseling, selective reinforcement procedures, and a placebo study group, and then post-test after the experimental procedures have been completed. In this case the test instrument becomes a criterion measure, the treatment procedures constitute independent variables, and changes in behavior and attitude reflected on the post-treatment scores become the dependent criterion variable measure.[8]

In all of the above examples of uses of testing, test constructors and research personnel would readily acknowledge that the test instrument itself is not the criterion variable but is an attempt to convert a complex criterion into some kind of measurable unit or units. However, the difficulty with testing usage centers very much on the determination of an adequate criterion which is independent of the testing instrument. Far too often the users of tests and even researchers have come to accept test scores as an ultimate criterion. In other instances because of the sophisticated procedures of utilizing factor analysis or many testing instruments we have tended to accept factors derived from such studies as criteria. In still other instances we have looked for overly simplified indices such as grade-point averages, achievement scores, and the like as the measuring sticks of behavior. *If the explorations into environmental assessment techniques mean anything, they mean that we must question seriously the notion that effective human behavior can be measured by a unitary criterion.* For there are quite evidently multiple sets of criteria which measure effective human behavior in different settings. This implication then has considerable impact on what constitutes a valid measure and even more impact on the traditional notion of reliability.

Astin (1965) discussed some of these matters in an article about criterion problems in testing. He pointed out that a criterion is essentially ecological in nature and is not contingent upon its relationship to any antecedent variable.

---

[8] This is an obvious oversimplification of a complex area of research design which is stated here only as an example of one use of testing in research designs. The reader is referred to Fred N. Kerlinger's book, *Foundations of Behavioral Research* (Holt, 1965), Chapters 16 and 17, and to the excellent chapter by D. Campbell and J. Stanley, "Experimental Designs and Quasi-Experimental Designs for Research on Teaching" in N. Gage, ed. *Handbook of Research on Teaching,* (Rand McNally, 1963).

In contrast to a purely psychological construct or trait, a criterion variable usually refers to a relationship between the person and his environment. It is, in fact, difficult to speak of 'standards' of performance or of behavior as being 'desirable' without also defining the social context in which the behavior occurs.

Astin indicts the effort of those who would set about creating testing instruments, standardizing them, and then assuming that the test score is the criterion of the performance. He points out that one of the most common misconceptions about criteria is that they can be "validated" through either intercorrelation procedures or factor analysis. It is also not sufficient that a given test correlate highly with another similar instrument. Though this procedure was used extensively in the past and still is common today, all measurement theorists recognize that what occurs is a shifting of the burden of validity to another instrument.

Because of the complexity of human behavior, normative information tends to smooth out individual differences and result in a bland profile which at its very least does not take into consideration the facts of creativity and cultural differences. This is particularly true in terms of personality testing and the testing results which have occurred for racial and cultural groups. These are two areas which should be examined further in terms of the implications which they generate for counseling and testing.

Personality Testing

Some of the shortcomings of personality testing are well known. They have been misused by a variety of individuals for purposes which are not too often delineated. Because of the assumption that the test score constitutes a criterion of performance, testing has often become an end to itself. The collection of many test scores is assumed to be better than a few indices, though Cronbach and Gleser (1959) have clearly pointed out that the personnel worker cannot keep more than a few selected variables in mind at any time when he is attempting to make decisions about people.

Recently a short book appeared on the subject of *How to Beat Personality Tests* (Alex, 1966). This little book is a short, amusing, but unfortunately accurate compendium of ways and means to beat the personality test. It is specifically written for individuals who are applying for jobs where a battery of personality tests is required. But incidentally, it provides an excellent critique and illustration of the implicit recognition of environmental press as derived from test scores. The first three chapters provide the justification for the publication of the book. The argument states simply that personality tests are often used by companies to screen applicants and that the scoring and use of these tests is often prejudicial to the applicant. The weaknesses of personality constructs and personality testing are labeled. Moreover, it is suggested that many of these tests are inadequately validated, possess little relevance to the job situation, and are frequently interpreted by personnel men who have had a "smattering of training" or by the "amateur psychologist retained by firms to test their applicants." The author of the book does not indict psychologists and psychiatrists who use tests within the framework of an interview with a view towards treatment, and he urges his readers to answer "all questions as honestly as possible" in these situations.

The general approach to the personality test which Alex advocates is to determine the nature of the stereotype or cultural model desired by the business. For example, the author describes the characteristics supposed to be associated with the accountant. An individual applying for such a position is advised to respond to all personality tests as if he were a shy, retiring, and methodical person. This methodical nature is supposed to transfer into one's social life, family relations, and sexual affairs. The accountant is judged to be a rather cold person, strong on logic, impervious to emotion, and with little sense of humor.

In personal matters such as sex, the author advises the test taker to answer questions from the most heterosexual point of view. In religion he is instructed to show some passing interest in the Church as a sponsor of "strawberry festivals" and supporter of the "Sunday School," but above all to show no interest in Bible reading, the social mission of the Church, or anything bordering on mysticism. Business executives do not want mystics and religion labels one as a mystic. In other personality tests, belief in the second coming of Christ is considered an aberrant response.

The balance of the book is concerned with specific tests and the proper approach to these tests. True-false questions are discussed explicitly from the point of view of social acceptability norms, with the directive to the reader being to respond in the most bland manner congruent with the social behavior desired. Word-association tests and sentence-completion tests are also discussed from this point of view. In the latter, the reader is instructed in the art of producing innocuous responses. For example, in response to the stimulus "My Mother," the author suggests the completion ". . . was a real homemaker." This kind of response, it is reasoned, shows a certain degree of sincere affection but avoids the possible Oedipal consequences and over-dependence of a response such as "was real dear to me." In response to the stimulus "I hate," the author suggests the completion

. . . "Communism" — for who could doubt the sincerity of this completion?

Details are provided regarding the proper way to make a self-rating. One should show oneself as a rather average person who has a degree of self-insight and understanding. It is well to indicate that you have had some problems (for this is considered self-insight) but also to convey the impression that you have solved these problems (which were minor anyway) and now function as a stable, creative, and socially-amenable person. In relationship to draw-a-man figures, the author suggests appropriate heterosexual drawings which are conventional in the best art form of which the applicant is capable. On "picture story" tests and "ink blot tests" the applicant for a job is advised to keep his responses down to a minimum of about three responses per card for the "ink-blots." It is suggested that he make interpretations largely relating to the whole blot and see a lot of pleasant human figures, or at least neutral animal figures, who are doing something uninteresting such as walking, talking, dancing, etc. In certain circumstances, such as in the case of a job requiring some creativity, the reader is advised to increase the number of responses which are seen per card.

What the writer of this compendium is stating is not new to most counselor educators and psychologists. Many of us have been saying the same things to students for years. Not that we are instructing them how to "beat the tests," but rather we urge them to understand the built-in biases of test construction. Frankly, this book ought to be read by all counselors and psychologists. There is still an overwhelming ignorance of the power and predictive validity of many so-called "personality tests." What this compendium demonstrates is the recognition of the fact of environmental press in the whole area of personality testing. In a way more succinct than pages of argumentation, it demonstrates that in the area of business, environmental pressures dictate what kind of a person is wanted for a specific job. Testing of this type may then penalize the creative individual. Creativity and the combinations of personality factors which might conceivably contribute enormously to a business enterprise are considered indicators of "way-out" behavior which is suspect. The conclusion is that personality tests *where used as explicit criteria of behavior* are actually penalizing both the applicant and the business.

Unquestionably, used in conjunction with counseling and behavioral observations, some of these tests may provide helpful information useful both to the counselee and the counselor, but used as immediate criteria of behavior they are highly suspect. Actually, one must concede that an applicant who wishes to obtain a certain position and passes tests designed to probe his personality, obtaining the position, is actually a stronger candidate for the position.

This use of personality testing for screening purposes points out a series of problems associated with this kind of testing. First of all, test scores seldom provide a basis for dichotomous judgments. This is true of achievement and intelligence testing and most assuredly of personality testing. Since the judgment expected of the psychologist who administers such tests to applicants is ordinarily one of pass or fail, the tests are hardly useful in this context. Secondly, most personality tests provide a series of measures about constructs or theorized dimensions of personality. Cronbach and Gleser (1957) point out the difficulty that attends any personnel worker who attempts to make decisions on a number of indices simultaneously. Moreover, Cronbach suggests that test users should always consider what they gain in relationship to the cost. Sometimes a brief screening device, even of low traditional validity, can provide much information at a low cost. Conversely, extensive testing can often serve to confuse. A third problem associated with personality testing is reflected in the norming procedure. Very often school administrators as well as business executives tend to compare the norms of their enterprise with that of another. A school superintendent will, for example, compare the distribution of scores obtained in his school with other schools in the area, making judgments about the comparative efficacy of his system against others on the basis of achievement scores. Lindquist (1948) lamented this process, pointing out that what is needed is a distribution of school averages rather than distribution of individual pupil scores. The same judgment is accurate for the use of personality profiles and norms based on clinical groups. Finally, the critique of personality testing provided by Alex demonstrates from the lay point of view the current concern which measurement theorists have with construct validity and response styles, both of which have been exposed repeatedly as factors limiting the interpretation and use of personality testing.

Cultural and Racial Bias

Another area where the environmental press is particularly well documented in testing is the whole situation regarding the testing of cultural minorities. Recently, Audrey M. Shuey (1966) published the second edition of a book entitled *The Testing of Negro Intelligence*. This volume is the most complete summary of research on the intelligence testing of Negroes. It documents the fact that American Negroes consistently score lower than Caucasians on all kinds of standardized group and individual intelligence, achievement, and motivation tests.

Negroes are consistently found to be lower on tasks requiring logical analysis, abstract reasoning, certain perceptual-motor skills, and non-verbal performance. There are more retarded Negroes and fewer gifted ones than in the corresponding Caucasian population.

In many ways Shuey's book reminds one of the current television repertory. There are many series which deal with inter-planetary explorations, earth invasions by aliens, mysterious dimensions of inner reality, and journeys through time. Every now and then a story develops in which earthmen land on alien planets. In one such story, the earthling is discovered by the aliens who look very much like him. They appear friendly and assure him that they are planning for his comfort. They then take him to a perfect replica of an ideal earth home. They evidently construct this by probing his brain memories in some way or another. Unfortunately, his joy is cut short by discovering that this home is in reality a new addition to the alien zoo. He is to be constrained to live out his days as a specimen of earth creature, and if perchance a female of the species can be obtained, the aliens might perpetuate the species indefinitely. In short, he and his descendants would then become a captive group of humans cultivated for the whims and purposes of an alien culture and thoroughly conditioned to a restricted outlook.

Shuey's book reminds one of similar conditions of the Negro in the Caucasian-dominated culture. Unfortunately, the realization of the poignant plight of the Negro in an alien culture is not fantasy. Shuey has amassed a vast kaleidoscope of research studies which have dealt with differences in testing between Negro and Caucasian groups. The studies are collated, analyzed, and summarized in gigantic tables. One can scarcely question the massive collection effort which has gone into this work. For example, in the chapter on school age children, one hundred and fifty-five investigations involving 35 different group tests and 14 individual tests are reviewed. These studies according to Shuey involve 80,000 "colored" children and include 539 Negro-Caucasian comparisons. This is typical of the overwhelming documentation and effort which is found in every chapter of this book.

Shuey systematically considers the research studies with young children, school children, high school and college students, the armed forces, veterans and other civilians, deviates, delinquents and criminals, "racial hybrids," and factors of selective migration. In every chapter, the majority of test results show that Negro scores are lower than Caucasian scores with an overlapping of means or medians of only about 10 to 12 percent. Studies are cited which attempt to control for socioeconomic class, sex differences, teacher differences in terms of level of education, and nearly every other conceivable variable.

The span of time of these studies is over 50 years, and though some are very old, others are recently completed. But they all seem to suggest in one way or another that no matter what is controlled or how favorable the conditions may be, Negroes obtain lower mean scores on testing instruments than do Caucasians.

This is the alpha and omega theme of the book: Negro test scores are generally lower than Caucasian test scores. In the foreword to the second edition Professor Henry E. Garrett, reviewing the book, suggests that though there is an overlapping of 10–15 per cent between Negro scores and Caucasian scores, Negroes at every age level and under a variety of conditions generally score lower than Caucasians. Garrett states: "We are forced to conclude that the regularity and consistency of these results strongly suggest a genetic basis for the differences. I believe that the weight of evidence (biological, historical and social) supports this judgment." Shuey in her concluding summary, which marshalls all of the conclusions derived from each of her chapters, concludes that these facts ". . . inevitably point to the presence of native differences between Negroes and whites as determined by intelligence tests."

This writer does not question the painstaking effort which Shuey has made in systematically collecting and reporting hundreds and hundreds of testing studies involving thousands of students and other comparisons. This in itself is a monumental task and is of value to the social scientist in reviewing cumulative test findings relative to Negro and Caucasian intelligence. Shuey tries to evaluate these studies as well, and sometimes her practice of lumping disparate studies together to obtain mean I.Q. ratings or mean scores may be questionable. It would appear that Shuey has established the fact that Negroes generally fare worse on testing instruments than do Caucasians. However, the conclusion towards which all of these data have been accumulated, i.e. native, hereditary and genetic differences between Negroes and Caucasians, is more than a little disturbing. Unfortunately, the racial differences hypothesis supports segregation and cannot help but breed controversy of the most heated nature. Somehow it is difficult for all of us to sort out the brutality of the Mississippi small town towards integration workers, the Biblical quotations distorted in support of segregation, from the conclusions of serious scholarly efforts which apparently support the same contention.

What this book does more than anything else is to demonstrate how profound has been the cultural deprivation accorded to the Negro in America. If racial differences exist, one should look at the chain of circumstances which surrounded the coming of the Negro to these shores and the treatment he has received over several hundreds of years. Questions which should be asked and investigated concern themselves with: 1) what kind of Negroes were captured and sold to slavers? 2) who died on the way over? and 3) how could survival be ensured? Certainly acquiescence was the key to survival. Moreover, the history of slavery, with its gross inhumanity to the integrity of the Negro family, its paternalism, and its systematic deprivation of education, cannot be overlooked. What can be said also in relationship to the constricted environment of the Negro in terms of modern research on environmental stimulation and cortex development?

The vast majority of social scientists tend to look at these differences as the result of a massive prolonged environmental deprivation. However, Shuey's book not by intent but by indirection points out that we should not expect instant changes as a result of massive Federal programs. Current efforts such as Head Start and the War on Poverty Program assume that cultural differences can be erased through environmental enrichment. The questionable results of some of these programs demonstrates that the Federal Government cannot erase cultural differences by quick, massive, and instant reparations. We shall have to persevere in such programs for many years before they will make a sizeable impact on cultural differences.

Dreger (1967) has posed an alternative that Shuey's thesis may be correct. He asks, "then is segregation a correct outcome?"

> Is segregation then the only answer to keeping a 'superior' race superior? (To say that segregation is also for the good of the 'inferior' race is at the best pure rationalization.) Is it the only implication that can be drawn from Shuey's thesis? No, not at all. Instead, the answer may be that the white race cannot afford to gain the whole world of intellect and lose its own soul. For to enforce segregation is no longer to be superior except in I. Q. points. The brutalizing effects of a system of segregation on both segregated and segregators are not worth keeping any race 'pure'.

Since the evidence of this book is based on test scores and testing instruments, one can see once again the impact of culture on testing. Nor is the Negro the only group who suffers from a bias in testing instruments. Some major cities such as New York City have come to suspect testing results seriously. Puerto Ricans and Mexicans also show poor comparative scores on traditional testing instruments. A recent Mexican study with the W.I.S.C. detailed the existence of separate sub-cultures for male and female groupings (Reyes de Ahumada, 1966).

Though it is not the purpose of this chapter to dwell on racial differences, it is pertinent to the general argument to discuss some unpublished research findings from the Oakland, California Public Schools Vocational Follow-up Study of 1965. This study involved nearly 3500 graduating seniors in 1965. They were tested on approximately 80 variables, including Holland's Vocational Preference Inventory, Farquhar's Motivation Scales, the California Psychological Inventory, and the Minnesota Vocational Preference Inventory. In addition a socioeconomic class scale based on Hollingshead's work was utilized. A number of interest patterns and preferences were also included. The data obtained in this manner is in the process of being analyzed and reported.[9]

Of particular relevance to the question of racial differences is a sub-section of the Oakland study in which 136 interest items were administered to all the students. Utilizing both the criteria of race and socioeconomic class, the responses were analyzed by computer. Only significant differences at the .01 level and better were identified in a chi square procedure. Hollingshead's socioeconomic index was used as a measure of social classification (1961). This index classifies socioeconomic groups on a I-V point scale, with I being the higher level and V the lowest level. Though significant differences of a large nature took place between the races when compared globally, the comparisons within socioeconomic groupings are interesting to look at. These differences are portrayed in Table I. Bear in mind that there were 136 possible differences.

Though considerable discussion could be presented regarding this table there are two major conclusions which the writer wishes to make in relationship to these findings.

1. The pattern of intercorrelations for racial groups and socioeconomic groupings indicates that standardized intelligence, personality, and vocational measures are highly influenced by cultural factors and that relevant analyses must be made in accordance with cultural groupings.

2. The factor of socioeconomic class structure is more central than that of racial differences. This is indicated from the pattern of significant differences. It is overwhelmingly evident that high socioeconomic groups have few differences in interest patterns despite racial differences. On the contrary, differences between Negroes and Caucasians in the lower socioeconomic classes leap to significant differences on almost half of the total items.

These findings support the contention of the writer that test scores as such should not be considered criterion measures in themselves but

---

[9] The Oakland, California Vocational Follow-up Study was directed by Dr. Robert Williams and Dr. Alden Badal of the Oakland Public Schools, with assistance and consultation in the research design and implementation from the writer and Dr. Thomas A. Soldahl, both of California State College at Hayward.

TABLE 1

Summary of Significant Chi Square Differences Obtained by Racial and Socioeconomic Groupings

	Female Distribution N Class and Racial Groups			Comparison Groups	Female Distribution Ratio of Significant Differences		
Race	I & II	III	IV & V		I & II	III	IV & V
Caucasian	171	289	396	Spanish vs Oriental	7/136	6/136	25/136
Negro	12	57	446	Spanish vs Negroes	2/136	8/136	31/136
Spanish	9	19	115	Spanish vs Caucasian	6/136	9/136	46/136
Oriental	11	24	41	Negro vs Oriental	7/136	15/136	35/136
Total	203	389	998	Negro vs Caucasian	17/136	32/136	62/136
	(High)	(Middle)	(Low)	Oriental vs Caucasian	4/136	11/136	13/136

	Male Distribution N Class and Racial Groups			Comparison Groups	Male Distribution Ratio of Significant Differences		
Race	I & II	III	IV & V		I & II	III	IV & V
Caucasian	132	265	417	Spanish vs Oriental	0/136	7/136	9/136
Negro	14	51	450	Spanish vs Negro	4/136	4/136	27/136
Spanish	3	23	117	Spanish vs Caucasian	2/136	6/136	18/136
Oriental	7	30	44	Negro vs Oriental	5/136	19/136	19/136
Total	156	369	1028	Negro vs Caucasian	7/136	20/136	59/136
	(High)	(Middle)	(Low)	Oriental vs Caucasian	1/136	11/136	7/136

must be taken in conjunction with the cultural criteria. Though cultural bias is well known to the constructors of tests, it is frequently overlooked by those who use tests and who tend to view test scores as criteria in themselves. In the areas of personality, intelligence, achievement, and motivation, as well as vocational dimensions, tests should be viewed and used only as indices of the relative standing of individuals within groups. Indirectly, tests reflect cultural differences and are therefore helpful in this respect.

Determining a Criterion Frame of Reference

If tests may not be viewed as criteria of effective behavior, what are they? Criteria of effective human behavior must be independent of the measurement device and usually socially oriented in terms of a specific cultural or environmental context. Generally speaking, appropriate criteria of effective behavior are related to the power structure within which an individual finds himself. The power structure ordinarily consists of individuals who are in authority over the individual and of peers who exert an influence on that individual. Thus, for a child in the elementary school the power of teachers and peers, as well as parents and other authority figures such as the Church, society, and mass media, all provide possible criterion measures of his conduct. His behavior is mediated by a complex system of reinforcements which are dispensed in accordance with his behavior. Effective behavior is judged by teachers in accordance with their subjective notions — which in turn are mediated by the system in which they operate. Thus, whether a given child is behaving in an effective manner is judged by the degree of correspondence between his behavior and the idealized norm towards which the teacher consistently or inconsistently shapes his behavior. A similar judgment is formed by the peer group where behavior is considered either congruent or non-congruent in a variety of contextual settings.

The research on environmental press has demonstrated the existence of differential criteria of excellence and performance in the collegiate and high school setting. Such "presses" are unquestionably present within sub-cultures of socioeconomic groupings. Racial differences also sponsor and support these differences. What is appropriate behavior for a Negro child in a slum is just as surely determined by his peers and respected adult figures as is appropriate behavior for the upper class Caucasian. Certain modes of behavior are developed and sustained, and the criteria of effective performance are found within the power structure of the sub-culture.

What does this mean to the counselor? *It means simply that in using tests as a means for improving decision-making, it is imperative to identify and recognize the explicit and implicit criteria of behavior which guide the behavior of the individual.* This can be done through a variety of procedures designed to determine more accurately the specific criteria operating in a given situation. Generally, what is sought is a clearer specification of the types of behavior which are acceptable and constitute effective behavior in a given environment. Hence, it is important in utilizing achievement tests to recognize what the operational and behavioral objectives of the school program are. Verbal objectives, even when enhanced with enlightened descriptions, are not always the real objectives. Teachers may be demanding certain kinds of behavior rather than other types. Thus, wherever possible, achievement testing should be matched to certain specific behavioral objectives.

A similar situation exists in personality testing. What is the relationship of certain personality dimensions to actual on-going behavior? Is there a correspondence between certain profiles obtained on a personality test and success or failure in a given situation? Perhaps a young man may show a highly neurotic profile on a personality test but yet be comparatively effective in dealing with peer groups. The same set of judgments is relevant to screening for employment in business. Again, what guarantee do we have that a pattern of interests obtained from a vocational inventory predicts success in a given vocation? Does a similarity of interest guarantee success?

In short, what is needed is to determine the correlates between test scores and on-going behaviors in a variety of social-psychological settings. The counselor cannot be expected to determine this completely on his own, but recognition of the fact that criteria of effective human behavior are contextual should provide a focus on the measurement of criteria which will make the use of testing a more relevant decision-making device. Moreover, with the aid of computer technology, the time is not far distant that reality-oriented criteria can be utilized in a more adequate manner. Individuals are constantly tuned into the reality criteria which operate in given situations. Group discussions among adolescents serve as one chief means of developing criteria of effective adolescent behavior. A similar function is performed in the more sophisticated T-groups or sensitivity training procedures for professionals. Students almost immediately grasp the nature of the learning climate in a teacher's approach to them. They learn what they can "get away with" and what kinds of demands will be placed on them. They also learn from infancy what kinds of restraints can be placed on them in the interaction of the family.

Criteria for effective behavior operate therefore in both inner and outer frame of reference. A large part of the counseling process is related to the determination of a psychological congruence between what an individual conceives his own personal criteria of conduct to be and what is contextually held in various environmental groups. Thus, criteria can be considered both from the subjective and objective frames of reference as well as from the individual and group points of view. To understand this notion better, perhaps the following diagram will clarify various sources of criteria. The diagram is constructed along two bi-polar axes, an objective-subjective continuum and an individual-group continuum.

FIGURE 1

Criterion Sources for
Effective Behavior Determination

Individual

Personal communication such as in counseling	Q Sort Procedures
Self-Report	Self-Concept Analysis
Autobiography and biography	Semantic Differential
Aspiration Level	
Spiritual Values	

Subjective — **Objective**
(Internal) **(External)**

Inter-personal relations and competency	External Behavior Ratings
	Teacher Evaluations
Approbation, Reinforcement Punishment	Power Group Evaluations
	Peer Ratings (Sociometry)
	Accomplishments (Recognitions, Listings, Extra-curricular activities)
	Promotions
	Achievement
	Systematic Behavior Observation

Group

Recognition of these possible criterion sources can help counselors to be more effective in their utilization of both testing and counseling procedures. Most of the items mentioned are self-evident, but it should be mentioned that the majority of social criteria are sustained through group procedures and therefore those criterion sources indicated in the objective-group quadrant are often the most powerful sources of criterion determination.

These listings of possible criterion measures which can be used to determine effective behavior in various contexts are not an all inclusive list; they are only suggestions as to possible sources of criteria. Many studies are needed to determine more adequate methods of criterion determination, within both the phenomenological and subjective realms and the objective and external frames of reference. The present status of knowledge about the nature of social behavioral learning in relationship to cultural transmission suggests that the cultural transmission is reflected in a variety of modeling, reinforcement contingencies, value judgments, and a continued flow of exemplary models in both the curriculum and interpersonal relations. This means simply that certain characteristics, personality, motivational, and vocational, are coupled with academic achievement in reaching congruence with criteria of effective human behavior. Testing can be a helpful procedure in delineating these personality, motivational, and vocational characteristics and in evaluating the progress towards a criterion, but testing is not a criterion in itself.

Generally, characteristics of a good criterion measure have been considered to be: 1) relevance, 2) independence, 3) reliability, and 4) availability. From what has been said thus far it is apparent that criterion measures are sustained by power blocks within the economic and social hierarchy of the culture and sub-cultures. Their relevance very often depends on contextual group settings which may not be identical to other group settings. Thus, it is not possible always to find criterion measures which are reliable over groups. They are highly relevant and independent of testing procedures, but in many instances they have been difficult to measure and therefore unavailable. Nonetheless, when one's son objects to wearing a pair of pants which parents feel are perfectly suitable, he is expressing a knowledge of a criterion of which his parents are not aware. The same is true of record purchases, ten-speed bicycles, and a thousand unnoticed preferences which have been shaped and molded by the peer group.

Implications for Counseling in the Secondary School

The recognition of the complexities of the criterion problem in counseling and testing is but one aspect of the larger problem of curriculum determination in education. Education in the 1970s and 1980s will include many novel notions. The behavioral goals and objectives of each student will form a new pattern of educational experience. Crucial to this experience will be the use of computers in memory recall and feed-back. Ideally, with the use of computers it should be possible to determine multiple criteria for evaluating progress in education and in the larger world of work. The present status of knowledge suggests that social behavioral learning is transmitted by the culture and sub-culture through a variety of modeling, reinforcement contingencies, value judgments, and a continued flow of exemplary models provided both in the school setting and out of it. Moreover, the criteria of effective human functioning are contained within the culture itself and are established by power blocks in the economic and social structure. Thus, the secondary school must provide a series of experiences which not only prepare students intellectually for one type of vocation but also provide the social learning base for the development of specific intellectual personal and motivational characteristics.

Unfortunately, we have been too addicted to a kind of half-truth, i.e., the education of the "whole child." This slogan has been considered for many years as the end goal of the educational process. It is surely recognized that individuals are intellectual, social, emotional, and personal composites and in this sense the "whole child" notion is accurate. However, from what is now known regarding the learning of individuals both in task-oriented intellectual learning and the social areas, it is apparent that individuals are collections of learned habits which include a variety of discriminatory judgments related to specific contextual criteria of behavior. A young man may be a lover to his girl friend, a recalcitrant to his parents, a popular guy to his peers, and a bum to the teachers. In some instances he may reflect highly contradictory roles as he moves from one environmental setting to another, casually or systematically meeting or failing to meet the criteria of effective behavior.

Parenthetically, it should be noted also that unfortunately a congruence in interest profiles does not necessarily spell success for a student aspiring to a given job. For testing results refer to constructs, traits, or factors which at the very best are hypothetical indices or derived factors. A series of criterion measures are needed which will determine, first of all, what constitutes effective human behavior in a given vocational setting, secondly, how the behavior of students aspiring to this criterion can be analyzed, and thirdly, how to determine the best way to help students shape their own behavior so that it is congruent with the criteria of effectiveness operating in a given field. Thus, for example, if John Smith wishes to be an electrician, what he needs to know are: 1) what kinds of personality, motivational, vocational, intellectual, and technical skills he may need to succeed as an electrician; 2) what his present deficits are; and 3) how a systematic plan of action can be developed to help him acquire these characteristics.

The development of such criterion measures, both in vocational education and the pre-collegiate curriculum, will require considerable time and effort as well as ingenuity. In the past the complexities of such criterion measures have made it difficult to take an expedient approach towards them. In part, it is for this reason that testing has been used so widely as a criterion measure or set of measures. However, with the availability of computers it should be possible to plot the individual learning curve of all individuals in a school, to determine what are the antecedents to those learning experiences, and to gradually help the individual explore his environment in terms of criterion measures or success characteristics. This will require numerous studies in which time sampling techniques are taken of behaviors typical and reinforced in a certain setting.

Thus, for example, it is not sufficient to know that skills pertaining to order, personality factors relating to reliability, consistency of behavior, etc. are required for a special job. What is needed is a determination of those actual behaviors which correlate with test variables (if tests are to be used) and which are congruent with success. The difficulties of obtaining adequate samples of effective behavior and the determination of base rates of such behaviors does not pose the difficult problem that it used to pose.

Cooley (1964) has pointed out that over half of the 19,000 high schools in the nation, serving some 9,000,000 students in grades 9–12, do not have adequate counseling resources for vocational decision-making. He has suggested that test data about individual students could be stored in regional computers and that with a systems-typewriter outlet in high schools, immediate access could be had to a computer. If computers could also store criterion data of vocational occupations, as well as of regional colleges and universities, in terms not only of global environmental "press" but of the specific departmental or divisional standards, it would be possible to provide information to individual students in a matter of minutes. The importance of computers linked in this manner to high schools is not only that adequate information could be had about individual needs in terms of risk-taking and decision-making, but information could be obtained about deficiencies. Thus, for example, if a student were interested in majoring in engineering, he might obtain specific answers to his questions about how well he could be expected to do at the state college in his area. Comparable data could be obtained for academic as well as vocational settings. Furthermore, if the computer could be consulted early enough, say in the sophomore or junior year, then a very powerful motivation could exist on the part of the student to increase his chances of success. Since it is now possible to store all kinds of information in a computer, why should it not be possible to include in this memory storage variables relating to effective criteria of personal, social, and curricular matters? In addition to answering specific questions about risk-taking, it is entirely possible that the computer might be able to provide information about the specific deficiencies that the student may have. Perhaps more work in algebra would substantially increase the probability of success in an engineering curriculum. Likewise, possibly the development of habits of regularity, responsibility, and order might be crucial to success in a vocational setting.

Another consideration is the fact that computers could provide programmed instruction tailored to the individual student. If specific weaknesses can be identified, the chances of success could be improved by the acquisition of additional knowledge or skills. A programmed course of learning in algebra could be guided by the computer. In addition, summer school programs could be used to obviate deficiencies as well as to provide supplementary enrichment experiences. All of these possibilities lead one to the conclusion that the use of computer technology in providing a "goodness of fit" approach to the criterion problem is a realistic and feasible way of increasing counseling effectiveness.

The use of computers in this manner is simply a reliance on technology to improve the quality of information available for decision-making. It is assumed that decision-making will be only as good as the communication and understanding of information which is available. As long as inadequate information is available in terms of the specific vocational questions that youth may ask, so long will the decision-making process be ineffective. Students do not really want to know how similar their interests are to those of successful people in a given field, but rather whether their behavior in all of its ramifications — personality, motivational, and technical — will enable them to be successful in a special field.

A further implication of computer usage is the manner in which computers promote the matter of learning decision-making. Bruner and Postman (1958) have pointed out that perceptual organization is powerfully determined by expectations built upon past commerce with the environment. This means that individuals can improve their own self confidence through successful practice in decision-making. The same is true of successive approximation to personality characteristics which are needed for success. A student knowing that he possesses

some characteristics which would obviate against success in a vocational alternative is immediately posed with the decision as to whether
he wishes to modify some of his personality characteristics or reject
the job alternative. Counseling can be helpful then in providing some
direct approaches to methods of personality alteration which will increase his chances of success.

Some may say that this sounds like a kind of "1984" approach to
human behavior. The difference is that computers and counseling can
provide both information and resources for individuals to appraise
their own ability in a realistic way, but there is no intent to force
compliance. One may argue against present standards of effective
behavior in given vocational and collegiate alternatives, but the fact
is that some degree of compliance to these criteria is necessary for
success. Without information specific to the situation, it is impossible
to pose realistic alternatives or methods of behavior change. In this
sense, then, the computer can become a possible source of information
which can be of great use to the counselor in determining both adequate indices of assessment and effective measures of criteria.

Implications for Counseling in the Elementary School

There is universal recognition that patterns of social behavior which
begin in the elementary school setting are sustained and developed
in later education. A central problem of the elementary school counselor or school psychologist is to determine who is in need of special
help in the learning process. The determination of this problem involves judgments about how these children can be identified, what can
be done in the way of procedures and techniques to effect behavior
change in children, and how to measure the effectiveness of the procedures and identification process. Any optimum attempt that the
elementary counselor may make to solve this problem should include:
1) a method of screening children in a comprehensive, economical,
and effective manner; 2) the use of procedures that can be used at
least indirectly in the classroom with the aid of teachers; and 3) a
means of measuring the change that takes place and evaluating its
success. The need, then, is to find not only appropriate means of
assessment and early identification of learning difficulties, but to
identify techniques that will bring about results.

One such procedure which can be of great help to the elementary
counselor is the systematic use of sociometric ratings and teacher
ratings taken in conjunction with each other. The two major sources
of criterion behavior in the elementary classroom are the peer group
and the teacher. These sources of criteria of effective human behavior

in the elementary classroom are extremely important, for they sustain the social behavioral learning within that environment. The writer in a series of studies relating to sociometry and teacher judgment has found that children with low sociometric and teacher evaluations are more prone to be impulsive and show signs of perceptual distortion (1965), show distinct patterns of interests (1966b), are more prone to drop out of school over a period of time (1966c), and are affected by the presence of male or female teachers in the classroom (1966a). In another study (1967), it was found that elementary personnel could effect changes in the social acceptance of given children in a classroom utilizing planned interventions.

All of these studies suggested that academic task-oriented learning is indistinguishable from social behavioral learning in the classroom. This is to say that all academic learning takes place in a social atmosphere, and the climate of that environment mediates the motivation, effort, and goals of children functioning in it. The studies of Kuhlen and Collister (1952), relating to the prediction of school dropouts through sociometry, and those of Kagan (1964), relating to the developmental patterns of elementary school children and their later achievement, leave little doubt that patterns of behavior which originate early in childhood and in the first years of education can continue to perpetuate themselves unless there is some active intervention. For social behavior which is continually evaluated by peer judgment and teacher reinforcement becomes an important mediating variable in the predominant task-oriented verbal learning of the school.

It is obvious also that desired changes in social learning behavior do not occur through desultory planning or haphazard attempts. If change is to be effected, it will take intensive study of the behavior of the individual in the group setting with a specific determination of the kinds of behaviors manifested by the child which are causing problems for him. This requires, first of all, an evaluation of those children who are potential or actual problems in the class through some kind of identification device. The writer has found that sociometric judgments and teacher judgments can be combined with an inventory based on Holland's rationale (i.e., realism, intellectualism, enterprising, artistic, and other dimensions).[10] This inventory provides information regarding the two major sources of criteria within the elementary classroom and also shows a sensitivity to differential environment "presses" which are operating within the classroom. Whether this specific instrument is used or not, the obtaining of teacher ratings for each child and sociometric ratings from the group can provide a considerable amount

---

[10] This instrument is entitled the Classroom Vocational Interest Inventory and is currently under development by the writer. Individuals interested may contact the writer.

of information for elementary counselors and school psychologists who are concerned about identifying children with learning difficulties.

The two measures can be plotted on a scattergram which yields information about the relative location of each child in relationship to teacher and peer group judgments. Figure 2 illustrates this scattergram arrangement.

Figure 2

Scattergram of Sociometric and Teacher Rating Judgments

	Low Teacher Rating	High Teacher Rating
High Sociometric	Quadrant 1 High Sociometric Low Teacher Rating	Quadrant 2 High Sociometric High Teacher Rating
Low Sociometric	Quadrant 3 Low Sociometric Low Teacher Rating	Quadrant 4 Low Sociometric High Teacher Rating

The four quadrants which emerge represent various combinations of teacher and peer judgments. Obviously, the more extreme position obtained by a child in one of the corners can be either a function of considerable concordance or disagreement between teachers and peers. From studies completed by the writer, it is apparent that boys who fit into the extreme Quadrant 1 corner tend to be impulsive, acting-out boys who amuse the rest of the class but harass the teacher. Conversely, boys in the extreme Quadrant 4 corner tend to be well-liked by teachers but disliked by peers. One such boy studied after a scattergram was made was a child who achieved highly, talked in a sophisticated manner about opera and classical music, but was living in a predominantly conventional environment where sports and dating were of more interest to his peer group.

Of more concern are those children who fall into the extreme corner of Quadrant 3. In one study done by the writer, over 900 children were followed for four years (1966c) to determine what happened to them. Approximately 54 percent of the females who dropped out of school and 64 percent of the males were in quadrant 3.

Such a scattergram arrangement does not, of course, provide any specific information about the behaviors which are occurring within the classroom environment and which result in the establishment of hostile or coercive behavior towards individuals. However, the pattern of choices which occur can be helpful in providing some real information to the elementary counselor or school psychologist about the manner in which the two major criteria of effective behavior are operating within a given classroom. Figures 3 and 4 provide some examples of the typical pattern of scores obtained from one relatively integrated classroom and one in which there is an obvious disagreement between peer and teacher judgments.

FIGURE 3   FIGURE 4

Well Integrated   Poorly Integrated

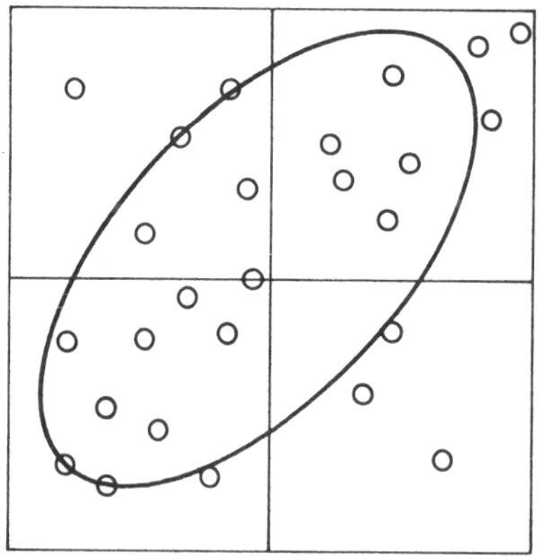

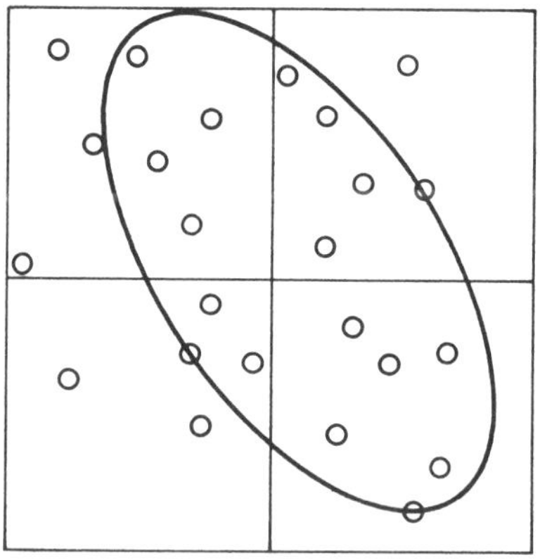

In Figure 3 teacher and students generally agree on their judgments concerning individuals in the classroom. In Figure 4 there is considerable disparity between such judgments. Such measures as sociometry and teacher ratings are valuable as criterion measures because they are relevant, generally independent of specific testing procedures, and appropriate to the environment in which the child finds himself constantly over many weeks and months of time. Moreover, they are easily obtainable. Though they are obtained on the premise that they will reveal the subjective judgments of both children and teachers, they are remarkably constant over periods of time, providing there is no active intervention. The converse is likewise true, i.e., that they are relatively good indicators of whether any change has taken place in the learning climate of a classroom. They can be used as criterion measures to evaluate the efficacy of intervention strategies used by elementary counselors and school psychologists. This was demonstrated in a study with three fifth grade classrooms in the Alameda, California, Public Schools (Barclay, 1967b).

However, it should be pointed out that such a criterion measure is helpful only as a screening device. These measures can be obtained easily, economically, and have a high degree of value for classroom teachers. Teachers have been uniformly enthusiastic about studying the composition of their own classes on these scattergrams. This access to teachers can thereby provide an avenue for the elementary counselor or school psychologist to do some in-service training with teachers and to plan further strategies for coping with certain types of behavior.

As a second step after the identification of children who need further evaluation, the elementary counselor should observe these children in their classroom and playground activities. A short behavior rating scale is helpful for determining those specific behaviors which appear to sustain a child's deviant responses or maladaptive behavior. If close attention is paid to the immediate antecedents of the child's behavior, it is possible to determine what led to certain kinds of respondent behavior and what kinds of operant behavior are being sustained by peer groups and teachers. Very often deviant response behaviors are actually sustained by the peer group and/or teacher.

Finally, a conference with the teacher can be scheduled in which her classroom behavior can be compared in relationship to effects obtained by one group of children as against others. The well-known bias of female teachers for female children is just one example cited here. Female teachers tend to be more supportive and nurturant for female children than for male children.

Intervention procedures can be designed and implemented by elementary counselors to help children who receive minimal social acceptance to learn new modes of behavior. This has been most successful when the interventions have been a part of the regular classroom experience rather than the summoning of a child out of the classroom by the elementary counselor for counseling. Actually, this latter procedure is probably more damaging to the child in the long run than not seeing him at all. For the appearance of the elementary counselor at the door of the classroom, the whispers to a teacher and the immediate departure of a problem child from the classroom set up a whole series of discriminative stimuli for the sustaining of even more deviant behavior elicitation by the peer group. In short, they know where he is going and why. Patterson (1967) pointed out that, in his experience with this type of behavior, students often redoubled their effort to continue the deviant behavior of the problem student in the same way they had done before.

Working within the setting of the classroom on a fairly routine basis provides the elementary counselor with an easy access to the group structure. If he regularly schedules a period or two each week or every other week to work with students in a given elementary classroom, his appearance can be paired with a rewarding break from routine. This is especially true if the elementary counselor is a male, for elementary boys are in real need of male counselors.

A few specific examples of procedures which have been found to be useful in the elementary classroom might be helpful at this point. Elementary counselors can often engage small groups of boys in hobby activities in which practice can be obtained in fine motor skills. He can also work out sociodramas which involve groups of children. In the study mentioned earlier (1967), sociodrama was used on several occasions, including the casting of low social status children in hero roles. One of the sociodramas related to the problem of a new boy with a speech defect entering a classroom and being teased. Another related to older students pushing fifth graders around on the sidewalk after school had been dismissed. In both instances the sociodramas were received with enthusiasm and a class discussion took place about the situations afterwards. The low status children were singled out for particular commendations in their role playing. Another technique used was that of a spelling game in which members of the team had to arrange themselves so that the word was correctly spelled. Several teams were used in competition and each team was composed of both high and low status children who had to work together to win. Small candy rewards were then passed out as rewards.

Other procedures which have involved groups of children have been tried successfully by Nixon (1967) and Beach (1967). Nixon found that children who are hyperactive, impulsive, and acting-out in a classroom not only disturb teachers but also other students. Building on this fact, he appealed to the peer group to help cooperate in reinforcing the behavior of an impulsive child. Utilizing a small electronic box which clicked for given periods of time for successful classroom behavior, such as paying attention, staying in a seat, or not interrupting a teacher, he gradually built up a repertory of new behaviors relying not only on the reinforcing agent and tokens awarded to the total group but on the massive social-reinforcement from the group. Beach, utilizing taped discussions of a small group of students regarding their lack of achievement, introduced small-group counseling to a model group. Over a period of seven or eight sessions, as the model group on tape came to grips with various problems relating to achievement and group attitudes towards both achievement and under-achievement, the model group made progress in resolving some of their own attitudes and behaviors. These tapes, consisting of ten-minute segments, were used to introduce similar group counseling procedures with children having the same problems. A separate model group of males was provided for males and a similar group for females.

These approaches to intervention in the elementary classroom which involve direct group or individual activities are related to some primary criterion behaviors rather than scores on a personality or achievement test. As a result, they are more directly susceptible to evaluation through systematic observation or rating procedures. A child who is disruptive in a classroom needs to learn how not to be disruptive. This involves not only the systematic extinction of maladaptive responses but the development of a new repertory of behavior which more approximates the expectancies of both teachers and peers. In the past, counseling has been more concerned with the appraisal of deviant behavior than the treatments used to bring about change. This has been in part the inheritance which counseling received from the medical model in psychology. Joined in this model was a strong reliance on tests and testing procedures to determine an objective approach to the measurement of achievement, personality, and vocational variables. Unfortunately, the union of these two strains produced a model for counseling which was strong on diagnosis and measurement but weak on a methodology for effecting change and for determining relevant criteria for effective behavior.

Summary and Conclusion

It has been the purpose of this chapter to focus on the specific problem of the criterion measure in counseling and testing. This problem is one of the persistent, important, and unresolved issues in both counseling and testing. Because it has been difficult to determine relevant, adequate, reliable, and independent criteria relating to effective human behavior, there has been a tendency either to utilize phenomenological constructs, such as self-concept or life adjustment, or to resort to a reliance on test scores as criteria. Though an argument can be made for the relevance of internalized and subjective criteria of behavior, the fact is that all of us live in a social milieu wherein our behavior is constantly being shaped and molded by cultural forces. We are a product of our experience and this experience is learned. What has been said in this monograph is that criteria of human behavior are sustained by the environment through a learning "press" which shapes and molds the perceptual apparatus of individuals through a variety of learned behaviors. Perception is both an active shaping force which influences the response repertory of individuals and at the same time the product itself of reinforced and operant behavior.

If behavior is cast primarily into a learning frame of reference, with special emphasis on the social psychology of group behavior, then the focus of deviant and maladaptive behavior can be sought not in instinctual forces but rather in a series of antecedent behaviors which have sustained and reinforced inappropriate behavior. This approach to school counseling will then result in a greater focus on social learning theory as it explains all kinds of inappropriate and maladaptive behavior. Consequently, the profession can then proceed to concentrate more specifically on the devising of strategies for reducing maladaptive behavior and building new constructive behaviors. This latter consideration is most important, for if we are to support new behaviors in children or adults, it is necessary for us not only to reason and clarify the old inappropriate behaviors, but to build positive new approaches to decision-making and responsible conduct. By considering more realistically what are the differential criteria of effective human behavior which exist in contextual settings, it is possible to determine what kinds of interventions ought to be undertaken by the counselor to bring about acceptable changes.

With the advent of computer technology, programmed instruction, and innovative approaches to teaching, it should be possible to determine more accurate criteria of behavior for given settings. In the school setting it is apparent that two major sources of criteria exist in the peer group and the teaching staff. In preparing for vocational careers it is likewise apparent that differential sets of criteria exist within vocations for effective success. In the collegiate and post-education world, still other sets of criteria exist which must be confronted if an individual is to develop personal habits of efficacy in coping with his environment.

The techniques and methodology for coping with these problems are just in a formative stage at this time. Clearly, much more research must be done to determine the precise methods which will have the most effect in changing behavior. This assumes that counselors will have to take far more responsibility for their actions than in the past. Where counseling was conceived chiefly as a reflective process, a minimal involvement could take place. It is relatively easy to schedule appointments once or twice a week to talk with individuals about their feelings. It is far more difficult to accept the responsibility of helping individuals change their behavior from ineffectual modes of thinking and behaving to more adequate approaches.

Finally, to return to the controversial problems relating to testing that were discussed in the first chapter of this monograph, the response to these allegations should be clear. Counselors and pychologists have tended to place far too much value on testing as an objective method of measurement. Further, they have implicitly, if not explicitly, come to utilize testing instruments as *de facto* criterion measures. A person has tended to be judged as neurotic if he had high neurotic scores. Though this fallacy has been recognized by measurement experts for many years, in view of the lack of adequate criterion measures testing has been used erroneously in many instances. As we develop more adequate criteria of behavior and more efficacious methods for both reducing maladaptive behavior and building efficient behavior, tests can be used in their true sense as normative measures based on objective procedures to aid in the decision-making process.

BIBLIOGRAPHY

Alex, C., *How to Beat Personality Tests.* New York: ARC Books, 1965.

American Capsule News, Sept. 15, 1962.

Ashbrook, John, "Brainpicking in the school." *Human Events,* Section 4, Nov. 17, 1962.

Astin, A. W., "Criterion-centered research." *Educational and Psychological Measurement,* Vol. 24, no. 4, 1964a, pp. 807–822.

————, "Personal and environmental factors associated with college dropouts among high aptitude students." *Journal of Educational Psychology,* Vol. 55, no. 4, 1964b, pp. 219–227.

————, "Some characteristics of student bodies entering higher educational institutions." *Journal of Educational Psychology,* Vol. 55, no. 4, 1964c, pp. 267–275.

————, *Who Goes Where to College.* Chicago: Science Research Associates, 1965.

————, and Holland, J. L., "The environmental assessment technique: a way to measure college environments." *Journal of Educational Psychology,* Vol. 52, no. 6, 1961, pp. 308–316.

————, "The prediction of the academic, artistic, scientific, and social achievement of undergraduates of superior scholastic aptitude." *Journal of Educational Psychology,* Vol. 53, no. 3, 1962, pp. 132–143.

————, and Nichols, R. C., "Life goals and vocational choice." *Journal of Applied Psychology,* Vol. 48, no. 1, 1964, pp. 50–58.

Ayers, L. P., "History and present status of educational measurements." *The 17th Yearbook of the National Society for the Study of Education; Part II: The Measurement of Educational Products.* Bloomington, Illinois: Public School Publishing Co., 1918, pp. 9–10.

Backman, C. W., and Secord, P. F., "Liking, selective interaction, and misperception in congruent interpersonal relations." *Sociometry,* Vol. 25, 1962, pp. 321–325.

————, and Pierce, J. R., "Resistance to change in the self-concept as a function of consensus among significant others." *Sociometry,* Vol. 26, 1963, pp. 102–111.

Bandura, A., and Walters, R., *Social Learning and Personality Development.* New York: Holt, Rinehart and Winston, 1963.

Barclay, J. R., "Approach to the measurement of teacher 'press' in the secondary curriculum." *Psychological Monographs (Journal of Counseling Psychology)*, Nov., 1967, in press, (1967a).

————, "Effecting behavior change in the elementary classroom: an exploratory study." *Journal of Counseling Psychology*, Vol. 14, no. 3, 1967b, pp. 240–247.

————, "Franz Brentano and Sigmund Freud." *Journal of Existentialism*, Vol. 5, 1964, pp. 1–36.

————, "Franz Brentano and Sigmund Freud: a comparative study in the evolution of psychological thought." Unpublished doctoral dissertation, University of Michigan, Ann Arbor, 1959.

————, "Interest patterns associated with measures of social desirability." *Personnel and Guidance Journal*, Vol. 45, no. 1, 1966a, pp. 56–60.

————, "Mobility, cultural change and educational leadership." *Family Life Coordinator*, Vol. 12, no. 3–4, 1963, pp. 97–104.

————, "Sociometric choices and teacher ratings as predictors of school dropout." *Journal of School Psychology*, Vol. 4, no. 2, 1966b, pp. 40–41.

————, "Sociometry: rationale and technique for effecting behavior change in the elementary school." *Personnel and Guidance Journal*, Vol. 44, no. 10, 1966c, pp. 1067–1076.

————, "Variability in sociometric scores and teacher ratings as related to teacher age and sex." *Journal of School Psychology*, Vol. 5, no. 1, 1966d, pp. 52–59.

Barclay, L. K. and J. R., "Measured indices of perceptual distortion and impulsivity as related to sociometric scores and teacher ratings." *Psychology in the Schools*, Vol. 2, no. 4, 1963, pp. 372–375.

Barr, D., "A note on the technology of cynicism." *Columbia University Forum*, Vol. 6, no. 3, Summer, 1963.

Beach, A., "Using audio-taped models in secondary counseling." Presentation, NDEA Institute for School Psychologists, California State College at Hayward, Summer, 1967.

Bedoian, V. H., "Mental health analysis of socially over-accepted, socially under-accepted, over-age and under-age pupils in the sixth grade." *Journal of Educational Psychology*, Vol. 44, 1953, pp. 366–371.

Berlyne, D. E., *Conflict, Arousal and Curiosity*. New York: McGraw-Hill, 1960.

Bidley, D., *Conflicts of Power and Culture*. Seventh Symposium of Conference on Science, Philosophy and Religion in a Relationship to the Democratic Way of Life. New York: Harper Bros., 1947, pp. 183–197.

Block, J., *The Challenge of Response Sets*. New York: Appleton-Century-Crofts, 1965.

Bloom, B., *Stability and Change in Human Characteristics*. New York: Wiley, 1964.

Boskoff, A., "Social indecision, a dysfunctional focus of transitional society." *Social Forces,* Vol. 37, no. 4, 1959, pp. 305–311.

Brentano, F., *Psychologie vom empirischen Standpunkt.* Leipzig: Meiner, 1873; Hamburg: Meiner, 1955.

Bruner, J., and Postman, L., "On the perception of incongruity: a paradigm." In David Beardsley and Michael Wertheimer, eds., *Readings in Perception.* Princeton, N.J.: D. Van Nostrand, 1958.

Cooley, W. W., "Computer system for guidance." *Harvard Educational Review,* Vol. 34, 1964, pp. 559–572.

Cronbach, L. J., and Gleser, G. C., *Psychological Tests and Personnel Decisions.* Urbana, Illinois: University of Illinois Press, 1957.

Dawson, C., *The Age of the Gods.* London: Sheed and Ward, 1934.

Dreger, R. M., "Hard-hitting hereditarianism." *Contemporary Psychology,* Vol. 12, no. 2, 1967, pp. 49–50.

DuBois, P. H., "A test-dominated society: China, 115 B.C.–1905 A.D." In Anne Anastasi, ed., *Testing Problems in Perspective.* Washington, D.C.: American Council on Education, 1966, pp. 29–36.

Ebel, R. L., "The social consequences of educational testing." In Anne Anastasi, ed., *Testing Problems in Perspective.* Washington, D.C.: American Council on Education, 1966, pp. 18–28.

Festinger, L., *A Theory of Cognitive Dissonance.* Evanston, Illinois: Row and Peterson, 1957.

Fifer, G., "Social class and cultural group differences in diverse mental abilities." In Anne Anastasi, ed., *Testing Problems in Perspective.* Washington, D.C.: American Council on Education, 1966, pp. 481–490.

Fishman, J. A., and Pasanella, A. K., "College admission-selection studies." *Review of Educational Research,* Vol. 30, no. 4, 1960, pp. 298–310.

Freud, S., *Collected Papers,* Vol. 4. London: Hogarth Press, 1953.

Gage, N., *Handbook of Research on Teaching.* Chicago: Rand McNally, 1963.

Goslin, D. A., "The social impact of testing." *Personnel and Guidance Journal,* Vol. 45, no. 7, 1967, pp. 676–682.

Gronlund, N. E., *Sociometry in the Classroom.* New York: Harper Bros., 1959.

Gross, M. J., *The Brain Watchers.* New York: Random House, 1962.

Guinouard, D. E., and Ryshlak, J. F., "Personality correlates of sociometric popularity in elementary school children." *Personnel and Guidance Journal,* Vol. 40, 1962, pp. 438–442.

Harcleroad, F., *et al., Learning Resources for Colleges and Universities.* An Advisory and Assistance Project No. OE–3–16–025, of the Educational Media Branch of the Office of Education, U.S. Department of Health, Education and Welfare. California State College at Hayward, 1964.

Hastings, J. T., *et al., The Use of Test Results.* Urbana, Illinois: Bureau of Educational Research, University of Illinois, 1960.

Hechinger, F. H., "Test Question." *New York Times,* October 27, 1963.

Heider, F., *Psychology of Interpersonal Relations.* New York: Wiley, 1958.

Holland, J. L., "Creative and academic performance among talented adolescents." *Journal of Educational Psychology,* Vol. 52, no. 3, 1961, pp. 136–147.

————, "Explorations of a theory of vocational choice and achievement, a four-year prediction study." *Psychological Reports,* Monograph Supplement, Vol. 12, 1963, pp. 547–594.

————, "A personality inventory employing occupational titles." *Journal of Applied Psychology,* Vol. 42, 1958, pp. 336–342.

————, "The prediction of college grades from the California Psychological Inventory and the Scholastic Aptitude Test." *Journal of Educational Psychology,* Vol. 50, 1959a, pp. 135–142.

————, "The prediction of college grades from personality and aptitude variables." *Journal of Educational Psychology,* Vol. 51, no. 5, 1960, pp. 245–254.

————, *Psychology of Vocational Choice.* Boston: Ginn and Co., 1966.

————, "Some explorations of theory of vocational choice." *Psychological Monographs,* Vol. 76, no. 26, 1962.

————, "A theory of vocational choice." *Journal of Counseling Psychology,* Vol. 6, no. 1, 1959b, pp. 35–44.

————, and Nichols, R. C., "Prediction of the first year college performance of high aptitude students." *Psychological Monographs,* Vol. 77, no. 7, 1963.

————, "Prediction of academic and extracurricular achievement in college." *Journal of Educational Psychology,* Vol. 55, no. 1, 1964, pp. 55–65.

Hollingshead, A. B., *Elmtown's Youth.* New York: Wiley, 1949.

Jackson, E., and Forsyth, F., "A comparison of upper elementary school children's responses on a vocational preference inventory and a semantic differential in relationship to a social desirability grid." Unpublished master's thesis, California State College at Hayward, 1966.

Kaufman, H., "Task performance, expected performance and responses to failure as functions of imbalance in the self concept." Unpublished doctoral dissertation, University of Pennsylvania, Philadelphia, Pennsylvania, 1962.

Kelly, G. A., *A Theory of Personality.* New York: W. W. Norton, 1963.

Kerlinger, F. N., *Foundations of Behavioral Research.* New York: Holt, Rinehart and Winston, 1965.

Kirk, S. A., *Early Education of the Mentally Retarded.* Urbana, Illinois: University of Illinois Press, 1958.

Kluckhohn, C., "The concept of culture." In Ralph Linton, ed., *The Science of Man in the World Crisis*. New York: Columbia University Press, 1945.

Kuhlen, R. G., and Collister, E. G., "Sociometric status of sixth and ninth graders who fail to finish high school." *Educational and Psychological Measurement*, Vol. 12, 1952, pp. 632–637.

Lee, E. S., "Negro intelligence and selective migration: a Philadelphia test of the Klineberg hypothesis." *American Sociological Review*, Vol. 16, 1951, pp. 227–233.

Lewin, K., *Principles of Topological Psychology*. New York: McGraw-Hill, 1936.

Lindquist, E. F., "Norms of achievement by schools." In Anne Anastasi, ed., *Testing Problems in Perspective*. Washington, D.C.: American Council on Education, 1966, pp. 269–271.

————, "Special Report on ACT Study of a method of scaling high school grades to improve the prediction of college grades." Mimeographed speech, Denver, Colorado, May, 1963.

Miller, W., and Swanson, S., *The Changing American Parent*. New York: Wiley, 1958.

Mowrer, O. H., Ellis, E., Curran, C. A., and Shoben, E. J., Jr., "The role of sin in psychotherapy." A symposium held at the Annual Meeting of the American Psychological Association, Cincinnati, Ohio, Sept. 4, 1959. Also reported in the *Journal of Counseling Psychology*, Vol. 7, no. 3, 1960.

Mussen, P. H., and Porter, L. W., "Personal motivations and self conceptions associated with effectiveness and ineffectiveness in emergent groups. *Journal of Abnormal Social Psychology*, Vol. 59, 1959, pp. 23–27.

Nixon, S., "Extinction of deviant responses in a classroom." Presentation, NDEA Institute in School Psychology, California State College at Hayward, Summer, 1967.

Osgood, C. E., Suci, G. J., and Tannenbaum, P. H., *The Measurement of Meaning*. Urbana, Illinois: University of Illinois Press, 1957.

Pace, C. R., and Stern, G. G., "An approach to the measurement of psychological characteristics of college environments." *Journal of Educational Psychology*, Vol. 49, 1958, pp. 269–277.

Piaget, J., *Origin of Intelligence in Children*. New York: International Universities Press, 1952.

Pulling, P., column in *Intermountain*, Pocatello, Idaho, Vol. 12, no. 43, Nov. 7, 1963.

Reyes de Ahumada, I., "Consideraciones acerca de la estandarizacion de pruebas a Latino-America, con illustraciones de la adaptacion del WISC a Mexico." *Revista Mexicana de Psicologia*, Vol. 2, no. 10, 1966, pp. 813–823.

Rogers, C., *Client Centered Therapy*. Boston: Houghton Mifflin, 1951.

————, *On Becoming a Person*. Boston: Houghton Mifflin, 1961.

Shuey, A. M., *The Testing of Negro Intelligence,* 2nd ed. New York: Social Science Press, 1966.

Super, D. E., "Vocational adjustment: implementing a self-concept." *Occupations,* Vol. 30, 1951, pp. 88–92.

Taylor, J. G., *The Behavioral Basis of Perception.* New Haven: Yale University Press, 1962.

Thistlethwaite, D. L., "College environments and the development of talent." *Science,* Vol. 130, 1959, pp. 71–76.

————, "College press and changes in study plans of talented students." *Journal of Educational Psychology,* Vol. 51, no. 4, 1960, pp. 222–234.

Tiedeman, D. V., "A model for the profile problem." In *Proceedings of the 1953 Invitational Conference on Testing.* Princeton, N.J.: Educational Testing Service, 1954.

————, Bryan, J. G., and Rulon, P. J., "The utility of the airman classification battery for assessment of airmen to eight air force specialties." Cambridge, Mass.: Educational Research Corporation, 1953.

Tindall, R. H., "Relationships among indices of adjustment status." *Educational and Psychological Measurement,* Vol. 15, 1955, pp. 152–162.

Wolf, R., "The measurement of environments." In Anne Anastasi, ed., *Testing Problems in Perspective.* Washington, D.C.: American Council on Education, 1966, pp. 491–502.

Wylie, R. C., *The Self Concept.* Lincoln: University of Nebraska Press, 1961.

ANNOTATED BIBLIOGRAPHY

Anastasi, Anne, *Testing Problems in Perspective*. Twenty-fifth anniversary volume of topical readings from the invitational conference on testing problems, American Council on Education, Washington, D.C., 1966.

This volume is a collection of lectures and discussions by noted authorities in the field of testing. It contains sections on test development, psychometric theory, and special problems in the assessment of individual differences. The book is a veritable collection of past and recent wisdom in the field of test construction, test usage, and test interpretation. It constitutes an excellent reference for students of testing.

Goldman, Leo, *Using Tests in Counseling*. New York: Appleton-Century-Crofts, 1961.

Goldman's book is a classic in the field of test usage for counselors. It is perhaps the most exhaustive treatment of the issues of using and interpreting tests woven into the context of counseling practice.

Kerlinger, Fred N., *Foundations of Behavioral Research*. New York: Holt, Rinehart and Winston, 1965.

For those who are interested in a very readable and yet sophisticated study of experimental design in counseling research, this volume is a must. Kerlinger's treatment of traditionally difficult topics is clear and unambiguous. Illustrations are provided which make it possible for the counselor with little background in formal statistics to grasp the basic notions of test construction and research design.

Megargee, Edwin I., *Research in Clinical Assessment*. New York: Harper & Row, 1966.

This is an excellent review of the research literature on testing, particularly in its clinical phases. The term clinical, however, should not disguise the fact that there is an excellent treatment of such topics as test construction, projective techniques, and a host of commonly used personality inventories such as the California Psychological Inventory, the Sixteen Personality Factor Questionnaire, and the Myers-Briggs Type Inventory. This book should be in the reference library of every counseling office.

INDEX